.

GROWING ON THE GO
DEVOTIONS FOR BUSY FAMILIES

RHONDA R. REEVES

New Hope Publishers
Birmingham, Alabama

New Hope Publishers
P. O. Box 12065
Birmingham, AL 35202-2065
www.newhopepubl.com

Library of Congress Cataloging-in-Publication Data
Reeves, Rhonda R., 1952-
  Growing on the go : devotions for busy families / Rhonda R. Reeves.
     p. cm.
Includes bibliographical references (p.   ).
  ISBN 1-56309-720-6
  1. Family--Prayer-books and devotions--English. 2. Christian education of children. I. Title.
  BV255 .R39 2002
  249--dc21
                              2002006105

Cover design by Righteous Planet

ISBN: 1-56309-720-6
N034104•1002•7.5M1

DEDICATION

This book is dedicated to my husband, Wayne, who keeps me on the go and inspires me daily to keep growing in God's Word; and to our son, Matthew, who we kept on the go constantly, yet still with God's help grew into the finest young Christian man I know!

Thanks, guys, for your love and support. You're both terrific, and I'll love you forever.

CONTENTS

Introduction

Busy families—they are a sign of the times! Look in your neighborhood; church; mall; schools; childcare centers; grocery stores; and, yikes, even your own house. They are everywhere. They signal an epidemic of the twenty-first century spreading rapidly from one household to the next.

Recently as I was driving, I pulled behind a minivan. When I got close enough to read the license plate, there it was. Another sign: VAN GO! I'm sure you too have seen these "signs" of families on the go, but have you stopped to consider how young children grow on the go?

If young children are to grow on the go, parents and caregivers must make sure that the child's physical, emotional, mental, and spiritual needs are met. Today's families seek only the best for their children. They want them physically well and active, so they have regular medical checkups and are involved in sports, wellness programs, and kiddie gymnastics. They want their children to be intelligent, so they seek the best preschools and interview teachers and school administrators. They are eager for their young children to socialize, so they sign them up for a variety of activities where other preschoolers are. They are also sensitive to their child's emotional state, so they are in the know about the latest issues in child development and psychology. Today's parents also want to help nurture their child's faith. However, many of them feel inadequate for this challenge and tend to lean on the church solely to satisfy this need. But a parent's role in his child's faith development is crucial. The most important thing a parent does to nurture his child's faith is to develop a loving relationship with his child. That relationship grows every day even on the go.

In her book *Joining Children on the Spiritual Journey*, Catherine Stonehouse reminds us, "Young children think deeply about God. . . . They want to know more about God.

The unseen God is real to children."[1] Parents should keep in mind that "we do not give children their primary understanding of God through formal religious instruction. . . . Rather we guide them . . . in the light of what they learn from us and in their ever expanding life experiences. . . . God becomes increasingly real to children as they have opportunity to participate with us in the living of our faith and in the worship of God spontaneously in the flow of everyday life."[2] Even if you are a busy parent, you can help your child grow spiritually while on the go.

Growing on the Go suggests fun, creative ways for preschoolers, aged three to five years old, to grow spiritually while on the go with their busy families. It is aimed to help preschoolers understand basic concepts of God and Jesus, God's Word, families, self, and today's issues. A simple devotional thought along with several hands-on activities and ideas will enhance a child's understanding and lay strong foundations for each concept.

A parent of a five-year-old sat next to me on the plane while I was working on this book. He asked what I was doing and when I told him, he said, "Well, I've always just winged it with my kid. Hopefully he'll turn out OK."

Well, I too hope he turns out OK. But being a responsible parent involves being prepared and ready to give clear, concise, and honest answers to your young children's questions about God. These are the most impressionable years in a child's life. As he grows on the go, what are you impressing upon him?

How to Use This Book

Using this book is as easy as 1, 2, 3. Make it fun and keep it simple! Although there is sequence to the book, you may find it helpful occasionally to select a devotional thought that pertains to a circumstance or event your child may be experiencing on a certain day. After you have read each devotion, talk about it with your child as you ride in your car, eat your dinner, take a walk, or while you sit and hold your child.

1. Parent Pointers at the beginning of each section suggest desired outcomes to work toward as your child learns about a particular concept.

2. Growing is a devotional thought for a parent or caregiver to read to his child. Many of the thoughts have been divided into several days' readings. These are marked as Day 1, Day 2, etc. After reading each thought, open the Bible and read the suggested Bible thoughts. Bible thoughts suggested in this book are Bible verses that have been paraphrased for a preschooler to understand. After reading the Bible thoughts, talk to your child about what they mean. Ask him to tell you what he thinks the Bible thought means. Then lead your child to pray. Use Say a Prayer as a guide, but encourage your child to say his own sentence prayers.

Depending on your child's age and development, you can decide how long to spend with each thought. You might like to repeat a devotional thought even two or three times since repetition is a way a preschooler learns. You can either read the thought to your child or tell it in your own words.

Answer your child's questions honestly. If you are not sure about an answer to a child's question about God, say: I really don't know the answer to that, but together we can try to find out. If you do not feel your child is ready to move to the next thought, continue to do more activities and have more discussions. Remember each child is unique and will learn at his own pace. Also remember that preschoolers are concrete, literal thinkers. When talking to them about God, avoid abstract ideas or terms.

3. On the Go suggests ideas and activities to use with the preschool child and family to help reinforce the devotional thought. Invite your child to choose one or several activities to do. Let a child do as much of the activity by himself as possible. Offer help only when the child asks for it. Praise the child for his efforts.

Thank you for loving and caring for young children, for nurturing their faith development, and for inviting God to go with you as your child grows on the go.

Part I
Growing in My Awareness of God and Jesus

PARENT POINTERS
- Lead your child to know that God is love, God is good, and God is great! Teach your child who God is.
- Help your child understand that God made a beautiful world for him to enjoy.
- Talk to your child about all the different kinds of people God made.
- Guide your child to know that God has a plan for his life.
- Lead your child to realize that God can do things that people cannot do.
- Encourage your child to talk to God.
- Lead your child to know that he can obey God.
- Help your child discover how he can worship God.
- Remind your child that he is important to God.
- Guide your child to know that Jesus was born, He grew, and that He went about doing good things.
- Help your child to know that He can be like Jesus.
- Read stories about Jesus' friends to your child.
- Point out that Jesus wanted to give love and peace to the world.
- Help your child to be aware that church is a happy place where he can go to learn more about God and His Son, Jesus.

Who Is God?

GROWING

Day 1—God is love, and He wants you to love Him. The Bible tells you to love God with all your heart, mind, and soul. That means to love Him with everything you have. God wants you to love others also. God lets you know how much He loves you in many different ways. Your mom and dad can help you know more about God and His love. Things in nature, like the warm sunshine on your shoulders, can do this too. When you help someone, and it makes that person and you feel good to do so, you can feel God's love. God loves you so much that He sent His Son, Jesus. Jesus came to teach the world that God is love.

Day 2—God is good. God makes sure that you have every-thing you need. He gives you good food to eat and clothes to wear. He gives you a family and a home where you can feel safe. Even though you may not see God, you can trust that God is always with you. When you play with your friends and you are happy, laughing, and having fun together, God is there. When you're sad, lonely, scared, or sometimes mad, God is there at those times too. The Bible tells us that God loves you and He will be with you. God is good.

Day 3—God is great. God can do things that people cannot do. He knows everything, and He has power that no one else has. God is the ruler of all things in the world. God is a mighty God and an awesome God.

So who is God? God is love. God is good. God is great. God is the ruler of all things. He is a mighty, awesome God!

Open the Bible, and read: God loves us always (see Psalm 107:1); God is good to us (see Psalm 73:1); God can do things that people cannot do (see Luke 1:37); and God loved us and sent His Son (see 1 John 4:10).

Say a prayer: Dear God, You are an awesome God! Thank You for Your love. Thank You for Your goodness. Thank You for Your greatness. You are the ruler of the world, and I thank You for sending Jesus to show me what You are like. Amen.

ON THE GO
•As you are on the go with your child, sing this song to the tune of "London Bridge."

God is love, and He loves me.
He loves me. He loves me.
God is love, and He loves me.
God loves (child's name).

God is good. He's good to me.
Good to me, good to me.
God is good. He's good to me.
Good to (child's name).

God is great. He's great to me.
Great to me, great to me.
God is great. He's great to me.
Great to (child's name).

God has a plan, a plan for me.
Plan for me, plan for me.
God has a plan, a plan for me.
A plan for (child's name).

•Encourage your child to give special hugs to you, other family members, teacher(s), and friends.[1]

•Help your child make a "special hug" by tracing his hands onto a piece of construction paper. Then cut out the hand shapes. Help him glue each hand to one end of a colored piece of sentence strip so the fingers on each hand extend outward. Make several different sizes of heart shapes from red, pink, and white construction paper. Cut these out. On each one, write one of the verses (from your Bible reading), and help your child glue these to the sentence strip. Encourage your child to take this special hug to someone, wrap it around her shoulders or waist, squeeze her gently, and say: "I love you, and God loves you too."

God Made the World

GROWING

Do you ever wonder how the world got here? A long time ago, before there was anything else in the world, God was here. There was only darkness, and God was alone. God wanted to make a beautiful world to enjoy.

God didn't have any special tools or equipment to make His new world. But, guess what? God didn't need any special tools. He simply said, "Let there be light," and there was. God continued to add to the world. He made the sky and earth; the ocean and dry land; and the sun, moon, and stars. He made lush green plants, sweet-smelling honey-suckle, bright colors of flowers, thin blades of tall grass, and trees with big strong limbs and trunks. God made birds to fly in the sky, fish to swim in the ocean, frogs to jump in the ponds, cows to graze in the meadows, and even tiny ants to crawl and work in mounds of dirt. He made people too. God looked at everything He had made, and He was pleased.

God made the world for you to enjoy. Thank God for His beautiful world.

Open the Bible, and read: God looked at everything He had made and He was very pleased (see Genesis 1:31), and God gives us things to enjoy (see 1 Timothy 6:17).

Say a prayer: Dear God, Your world is a beautiful place filled with plants, animals, people, and good things to enjoy. Help me to remember that You gave me this world to enjoy. Thank You for giving my family and me such a beautiful world. Amen.

On the Go

- Take a nature walk or hike around a walking trail. Point out all the good things God gives you to enjoy. Collect nature items. At the end of the walk, talk about each item you've collected. Take the items home and make a mobile. Tie each item to a piece of string. Then tie the other end of the string to a hanger. Hang the mobile where you and your family can see it each day. Thank God for good things He gives you to enjoy.
- Make a bug catcher. Use a clean bleach bottle and cut off the top. Cut several "windows" in the bottle large enough that your child's hand can fit inside. Help your child collect fireflies, butterflies, crickets, or ladybugs to place in the bottle, and observe. Cover the bottle by wrapping the leg from old, clean panty hose around it. Gather the panty hose at the top and secure with a twist tie.
- Help your child learn this fun song to sing as you're on the go. Sing to the tune of "Do Re Mi."

> *God, He made the world for me.*
> *Flowers, green grass, and the tall trees.*
> *The stars that twinkle in the sky at night.*
> *The sun that shines and is so bright.*
> *The sea and the land that is dry.*
> *Fish to swim, the birds and bees to fly.*
> *The cows to graze in the meadow.*
> *Thank You, God, for your world—we love it so-o-o-o-o-o-o!*

God Made People

GROWING

Day 1—After God made the heavens and the earth, He decided to make people too. God took a small amount of dirt from the dry land, and He made a man. God breathed His own breath into this man and then the man was alive. God was so excited to have created the first man. God told the man that He made him exactly like He wanted.

God made the man able to think and love. God gave the man a beautiful garden in which he was to live. God told the man to enjoy the beautiful world He had created. The man was very happy.

But soon God thought that the man was lonely. He wanted him to have a friend, someone to talk to, a partner to share his life with. So God made a woman to be the man's friend. The man fell asleep and when he woke up, there was a woman next to him. God had made a woman to be the man's friend.

Day 2—Can you imagine how surprised the man must have been when he woke up and saw the woman next to him? The man and woman were happy to be friends. They were glad that they could share God's beautiful world with each other.

These were the first two people. The man was Adam and the woman was named Eve. God continued to make more and more people. God made all kinds of people too. He made people with light skin and people with dark skin. He made people with blue eyes, brown eyes, green eyes, and black eyes. God made all the people in the world, and God loves each one of them very much.

Open the Bible, and read: God made people (see Genesis 1:27);

God made man (see Genesis 1:27); God made woman (see Genesis 1:27); and God made me (see Psalm 139:14).

Say a prayer: Thank You, God, for making people. Thank You, God, for making me. Teach me to be more like You in all that I do and say. Help me to love all kinds of people. Amen.

ON THE GO
- Cut out pictures of different kinds of people from a magazine. Help your child glue the people pictures to craft sticks and use them as puppets. Lead the conversation as the puppets "talk" about how they are alike and how they are different. Conclude the conversation by reminding your child that God loves each person and made each person special.
- Visit the library and check out a book about all kinds of people.
- Have a Family Fashion Show where family members "model" what makes them unique and special.
- Help your child notice different kinds of people you see at the mall, the grocery store, in a restaurant, at preschool, at church, or at the ball field. Talk about how people are alike and how they are different. Remind your child that God made all the people and that God loves them too! Pray for all of the people you see.

God Has a Plan Just for You!

GROWING

Day 1—Isn't it good to know that God cares for you? God loves you very much and He has a plan for your life. He wants you to be part of His plan.

Once there was a Hebrew woman named Jochebed. Soon after she gave birth to her son, she did something that most mothers would never do. Jochebed and her daughter, Miriam, put the baby in a basket and sent him floating down a river. They did this to protect him from a very bad Pharaoh (an Egyptian king). This king wanted to kill all Hebrew baby boys because he was afraid that there would be more Hebrew people than Egyptian people. So he sent out an order for his soldiers to search all Hebrew homes, find the baby boys, and then drown them in the river. The Hebrew people tried very hard to hide their babies. But when the babies cried, the soldiers heard them. So the soldiers found most of the Hebrew babies. But they did not find Jochebed's baby.

Day 2—Jochebed and Miriam watched as their baby went floating down the river. They couldn't believe what happened next. Pharaoh's daughter found the baby! She decided to keep the baby. Miriam knew that the princess would need special help caring for the baby, so she ran up to the princess. Miriam told her that she knew the perfect person to care for the baby. That person was Jochebed, the baby's real mother! God had a plan for the baby's life.

Day 3—Jochebed took care of the baby. One day as she rocked him, she said, "Little one, soon you will grow up. God will use you in a very special way. I know God has a plan for your life. He has protected you and saved you."

Jochebed was right. The baby grew up. When he was

older, the princess gave him the name of Moses. That meant "I got him from the water." Moses grew up to be a strong and great leader for the Hebrew people. Moses trusted God. Moses followed God's plan for his life.

You can trust God with His plan for your life too. Even when things seem scary and you may not know exactly what to do, God knows what is best. He will care for you. God has a special plan for your life just like He did for Moses' life.

Open the Bible, and read: God cares for you (see 1 Peter 5:7). For further reading, read Exodus 1 and 2. (Note: Read small sections of the story each day, as it is too long for a pre-schooler to sit through at one reading.)

Say a prayer: Dear God, How good it is to know that You care for me and that You have a plan for my life! As I grow, show me Your plan. Help me to trust You even when I'm afraid and don't know what to do. Amen.

ON THE GO

- Look through old photo albums with your child; share photos of yourself as a child. Look at photos of everyone in the family. Talk about ways God has worked in each stage of your lives and how He has used certain events to show you what His plan is. (Note: Do not overwhelm your child with too much information. Share bits and pieces along the way.)
- As you are on the go, play a rhyming game of "I'd Like to Be . . .". Ask your child: "Would you like to be a doctor?" Then the child can answer: "I could be a doctor. Yes, that's for me! A doctor helps sick people. Is that God's plan for me?" Continue with: "Would you like to be a leader like Moses? Would you like to be a teacher?" The child can respond to each question.
- Remind your child daily that God has a plan for his life and that he can trust God to care for him.

Wow! Look What God Can Do!

GROWING

Day 1—God made people and they can do many wonderful things. But God can do things that people cannot do. God knows everything and can do anything, even things that are beyond what you imagine.

Pharaoh, the Egyptian king, did not like the Hebrews. He made the Hebrews into slaves, and this made the Hebrews very sad. They did not want to live like slaves. They wanted to be free. So Moses helped the Hebrew people. He told them to get ready to leave and to follow him. He said with God's help, they would one day be free. So Moses and the Hebrews trusted God, and they began their long journey.

Day 2—Pharaoh was very angry when he heard that Moses and the Hebrews had left. He sent his army after them. The army chased the Hebrews for many days, but the Hebrews were able to stay just ahead of the army. One day the Hebrews came to a big sea. They had nowhere to go to escape from the army. They were scared and afraid for their lives. "Surely we will be captured and killed," they cried out to Moses. "We will never be free."

Moses called to God for help. And God did something that no person could ever do. He sent a very strong wind and that wind caused the water in the sea to part. The people were amazed at what they saw. "Hurry!' exclaimed Moses. "Let's cross over while we can."

So the Hebrews safely crossed to the other side of the sea. When they looked back, there was Pharaoh's army. As the army started to cross, the waters fell down all around them, and the army was drowned. The Hebrew people thanked God for saving them.

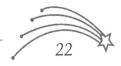

Open the Bible, and read: God can do things that people cannot do (see Luke 1:37). For further Bible reading, read Exodus 14:14–31.

Say a prayer: God, You can do great things that people cannot do. Thank You for being such an awesome God! Amen.

ON THE GO

- Provide your child with an easel, tempera paints, paintbrushes, and a big sheet of white paper. Lead your child to paint a picture showing the sea parting and the Hebrews crossing. Display your child's artwork in a prominent place in your home. Talk about things God can do that people cannot do.
- Go outside and use sidewalk chalk to work together as a family to illustrate the Hebrews crossing the sea.
- If possible, gather friends and family members to make a bulletin board at church to show that God Can Do Things That People Cannot Do! Be sure to include preschoolers in this activity.

I Can Talk to God

Day 1—God loves you and He wants you to love Him too. One way you can show your love to God is to talk to Him. Yes, that's right. You can talk to God! When you talk to God, you are praying.

You can talk to God about anything. God likes it when you tell Him what a great God He is. He also likes it when you tell Him about things you have done that you know deep inside you should not have done. God wants you to thank Him for all the things He gives you to enjoy. He wants you to pray for others also.

You can praise God, you can tell God about things you did that were wrong, you can thank God, and you can ask God to help you and your friends. How exciting to know that you can talk to the ruler and maker of all things!

Day 2—How exciting it is that God listens when you talk to Him! He will forgive you when you do something wrong. He will let you know what you should do, and He will help others for whom you pray.

God keeps His promises. He promises that He will always be there for you. So start right now. Tell God how you feel, what you are thinking, and ask Him to help your friends and family. Talk to God! He's always ready to listen.

Open the Bible, and read: Pray for one another (see James 5:16); call out to God, and He will hear you (see Jeremiah 33:3); if we tell God what we have done wrong, He will forgive us (see 1 John 1:9); and in everything give thanks to God (see 1 Thessalonians 5:18).

Say a prayer: Dear God, I am so glad that I can talk to You. Thank You for being there to listen to me. When I do things

that I shouldn't, please forgive me. Thank You, God, for everything You give me. Help my friends and family to know how much You love them. Amen.

ON THE GO

• Make prayer a priority for your family. Pray together at meals, even when you are at a restaurant or eating in your car. At mealtimes, ask each person to make one statement to or request of God.

• Pray before going to bed, while taking a walk, after reading a favorite book, or riding in the car to preschool or child-care. Find things that you can praise God for, and lead your child to do the same. Share concerns that are appropriate for your child, and lead your child to pray about them. Say thank-you prayers during the day with your child. Keep prayertime with your young child brief; and use short, simple sentence prayers as you lead him to pray. Avoid forcing a young child to pray out loud.

I Can Obey God

GROWING

Day 1—God wants us to do the right things. God tells us in His Word, the Bible, what the right things are. Later you will learn about God's Ten Commandments. You will also learn how you can live your life like Jesus. When you live your life like Jesus, you make God happy. When you do the things that God wants you to do, not only will God be happy about what you do and say, but you will feel very happy too. God wants everyone to live life in a way that pleases Him.

Day 2—Sometimes it's hard to know the right things to do. If you make a mistake and do the wrong things, God still loves you. God will always love you no matter what you do. God wants you to learn from the mistakes you make. If you keep trying to do the right things, God will help you. That's because God cares for you. If you do the wrong things and you know you are doing them, God is sad. But still He loves you. God wants all of His children to do the right things. That way God can bless His children with much happiness and joy. Obey God and show Him how much You love Him!

Open the Bible, and read: God takes care of those who hear His Word and obey it (see Luke 11:28).

Say a prayer: Thank You, God, for loving me, even when I do the wrong things. I want to do what Your Word teaches me. Teach me Your ways, and I will do my best to obey them. Amen.

ON THE GO

•Invite your child to help you make an I Can Obey God flip booklet. Give him seven 4-by-6 notecards. Provide crayons or markers. On one card write the title, *I Can Obey God.* Lead your child to put a decorative border around the title and to write his name underneath it. On each of the other cards, ask him to draw one way he can obey God. Help your child write a short sentence underneath each illustration. Laminate or cover the cards with self-adhesive plastic for added durability. Punch two holes at the top of each notecard in the same place. Use metallic or plastic rings to attach the cards together to make a booklet. Read the booklet together after dinner, before bedtime, or while enjoying a picnic at the park. When your child has finished with the booklet, take it to a children's hospital, preschool class at your church, or to a pediatrician's office where other preschoolers might enjoy reading it.

Look at Me!
I Can Worship God!

GROWING

Day 1—*Worship.* You might have heard your parents or someone use this word before, but do you know what it means? Worship means to honor God, to love God, to adore God, to praise God. When you do these things, you are worshiping God. God is a mighty God who wants you to worship Him.

Day 2—*Where can you worship God?* You can worship God at home, at church, at preschool, on the playground, in your room alone while playing with your toys, at the park with friends, and on the soccer field. You can worship God even when you are riding in your car.

When can you worship God? You can worship God anytime and, hopefully, all the time. No matter if it's morning, noon, or night, you can worship God.

Day 3—*How can you worship God?* You worship God when you show love and kindness to others. When you sing songs about God, you worship Him. When you pray, read your Bible, and go to church and listen to your teachers and pastor, you worship God. When you close your eyes and think about all the good things God has given you to enjoy, you worship Him. When you thank God for His beautiful world, you worship Him.

Open the Bible, and read: Shout joy to the Lord! Serve the Lord and be glad about it. Come before Him with joyful songs and know that He is God. It is God who made us and we are His people. Thank Him and praise His name. For God is good and He will love us forever (see Psalm 100).

Say a prayer: God, I want to show You how much I love You. Whether I'm at home, preschool or kindergarten, church, or with my friends on the playground, help me to show You how much I love You. Amen.

ON THE GO

•Make time each day for you and your child to worship. Gather the family together for a time of prayer and Bible reading. Sing songs, and praise God for His goodness. Your worship times can be before or after meals, before going to bed, or even while riding in your car.

•At church, welcome preschoolers into the church service, if only for a short while. Begin teaching them about worship and encourage your church staff to include young children in worship.

•Talk to your child daily about how he can worship God. As you are riding in the car or taking walks, look at the beautiful mountains, oceans, rivers, and valleys God has made. Let your child hear you praising God with a song, a prayer, or a poem. Keep a Bible in your car. Read favorite verses to your preschooler while waiting in traffic or while sitting in the car as you wait for older children to finish a piano lesson or a ball practice.

Look Who's Important to God—I Am!

GROWING

Day 1—God loves you so much that He sent His Son, Jesus. Jesus came to the world so you could know more about God's love. God sent you, your family, and friends the greatest gift of all—His one and only Son, Jesus.

Jesus loves all the children of the world. It doesn't matter what they look like, where they live, or who their parents are. Jesus loves everyone the same.

You are very important to Jesus. Jesus wants you and all the little children of the world to know about Him and all the good things He did. He wants you to know that He loves you very much.

Day 2—Little children are very important to Jesus. One day, Jesus' friends who traveled with Him were fussing about who was the greatest among them. Jesus sadly shook His head in disappointment. Then Jesus saw a little child playing. He picked up the little child and placed him on His knee. Jesus asked His friends, "Do you see this little child? The greatest person is the one who can become like this little child. This little child is trusting, loving, and kind."

Jesus' friends were surprised at what He had said. But Jesus wanted them to learn a very important lesson about how they should relate to God. Jesus saw in children many good and important things. He taught adults that they could learn a lot from children. Children were important to Jesus. You are important to God. You are important to Jesus too.

Open the Bible, and read: Jesus said, "Let the little children come to me" (see Matthew 19:14).

Say a prayer: Dear God, thank You for sending Jesus to love me. I am glad that I'm important to Jesus. That helps me know that I'm important to You too. Help me to be more like Jesus every day. Amen.

On the Go

•Using an instant camera, take photos of your child playing, looking at a book, eating dinner, going to church, hugging a friend, etc. Invite your child to help you place the photos in a photo album. On the cover of the album, write, *Look Who's Important to God!* Each day continue adding photos to the album. Write captions for the pictures and share these at special family gatherings or during a mealtime.

•Help your child make a headband. Give him a sentence strip, and ask him to decorate the strip with drawings of himself. In the center of the strip, glue a photograph of your child. Around the strip write, *I'm Important to God!* Fit the child's headband to his head, and staple or tape the ends together. Encourage your child to wear his headband. (If you use staples, cover them with colored duct tape to prevent your child from getting a staple in his hand or head.)

Baby Jesus Is Born!

GROWING

Day 1—A long time ago a young woman named Mary and man named Joseph took a trip to a city called Bethlehem. They had traveled quite a long way and when they arrived in Bethlehem, they were tired and needed a place to stay. Joseph knocked on the door of an innkeeper's house.

"Hello," greeted Joseph. "My wife is about to have a baby and we are tired from our travels. Do you have a room where we could spend the night?"

"Oh, I'm sorry, but I don't have a room for you," said the innkeeper. "There are many travelers in Bethlehem tonight and all the rooms are taken. I do have a stable out back where the animals stay. You could stay there if you like," the innkeeper offered.

Joseph and Mary decided to stay at the stable. They were much too tired to keep looking for a place to stay. The cows mooed. The sheep said baa. Mary and Joseph settled in and that very night Jesus was born.

Day 2—Mary laid Baby Jesus in a manger filled with hay. No one in Bethlehem knew that this was God's Son who would be the Savior of the world. So God sent an angel to some shepherds to tell them the good news. The angel said, "Christ the Lord has been born. You will find Him in a stable lying in a manger. Go see Him, and hurry."

Then the angels started to sing, "Glory to God!"

The shepherds quickly went to see Baby Jesus. They were so excited to see the tiny baby. They thanked God for sending the baby. They knew that Jesus would grow up to be their Savior. Now everyone would know that God had not forgotten His people. God sent Jesus, His Son, to show people how much He loved them.

Open the Bible, and read: Jesus was born in Bethlehem (see Matthew 2:1).

Say a prayer: Dear God, thank You that Jesus was born. Thank You that the angels came to help people know that this baby was special. He was God's Son. Thank You for sending Jesus to show us how much You love us. Amen.

ON THE GO

- Although it may not be Christmastime, read the Christmas story this week to your child (see Luke 2:1–20). Since this is a long reading for a preschooler, read only a few verses at a time.
- Guide your child to set up the family's Nativity set with all the figures. Talk about the birth of Jesus as your child puts the figures in place around the stable.
- Help your child draw or paint the Nativity scene, or give him some play dough and help him make his own Nativity figures. Lead him to make a stable using a shoebox, straw or hay, glue, and construction paper. Glue the hay to the box to make it look like a stable. Then cut a star from construction paper. Bend down one point of the star and glue it to the top of the box so that it stands up. Place the dough figures inside the stable.

Jesus Grew

GROWING

Day 1—Just like you are growing every day, Jesus grew too. When Jesus was a young boy, He enjoyed helping Joseph, His dad. Joseph was a carpenter in the town of Nazareth. Together, they would work at Joseph's carpentry shop. They made all kinds of things out of wood. Jesus would hand Joseph the tools, and Joseph would make chairs, tables, and shelves.

At home, Joseph and Mary taught Jesus about God. Jesus loved hearing stories about God. He would sit with His parents and listen for long hours as they told Him about God. Jesus knew so much about God, and He was just a boy.

Day 2—One day Mary and Joseph lost Jesus. They searched for days looking everywhere, but they couldn't find Him. They were worried, just like your parents would be if you got lost. Then Mary and Joseph went to the Temple. Joseph looked up and saw a group of teachers gathered and listening to someone. Who were they listening to? It was Jesus! He was sitting right in the middle of the group of teachers. He was telling them what He knew about God, and the teachers were very impressed!

"Where have you been, Jesus?" asked His worried mother.

"Why, right here in the Temple," said Jesus. "Didn't you know I'd be here? I want to be here learning more about God."

Day 3—Joseph and Mary took Jesus home from the Temple. As they left, many people were wondering how such a young boy could know so much about God. They didn't know He was God's Son. But they were amazed at how much Jesus knew.

Joseph and Mary were proud of Jesus. He was a good boy. Jesus kept growing and growing. Jesus grew to be a strong man.

Open the Bible, and read: Jesus lived in Nazareth (see Matthew 2:23), and Jesus grew and became a strong man (see Luke 2:40).

Say a prayer: Dear God, thank You for Jesus. Thank You for helping Him to grow and become strong. Amen.

ON THE GO

•Let your child work with wood like Jesus did in Joseph's carpentry shop. Provide small pieces of wood scraps, sandpaper, white glue, paint, scrap materials (buttons, ribbon, fabric, yarn, etc.), hammer, nails, screwdriver, and screws. Help your child use the sandpaper to sand the rough edges of the wood pieces. Older preschoolers will enjoy hammering the nails to join the wood pieces together. (Supervise preschoolers very carefully when using these supplies.) Younger preschoolers can use the glue to hold the pieces. Help your child paint and decorate his creations. As you work, talk about ways Jesus helped Joseph in the carpentry shop.[3]

Good Things Jesus Did

GROWING

Day 1—Jesus grew into a man who wanted to tell everyone about God's love. Jesus wanted to show others that He loved them just as God did. So Jesus did good things to help the people learn about God.

Jesus prayed. Jesus prayed when He was alone and when He was with others. He talked to God about everything, and He listened to what God told Him. He obeyed God.

Jesus went to church. His church was called a temple. When Jesus was young, He went to church with His family. Mary and Joseph took Jesus to the Jewish Temple where He learned about God. As Jesus grew, He continued to go to the Temple. The Temple was one of Jesus' favorite places.

Jesus taught people. Even as a young boy Jesus taught the teachers in the Temple. They were surprised at how much Jesus knew about God.

Day 2—As a man, Jesus traveled to many places. Everywhere He went large crowds of people came to hear what He was saying about God. Jesus told stories to help the people know how to live their lives in the right way. Jesus told the people to love others, help others, and pray for others. Jesus told the people that He loved them and that they were His friends.

Day 3—Jesus did things that people cannot do. These things are called miracles. Once Jesus calmed a storm on the Sea of Galilee. Jesus and His friends were fishing on a boat when a terrible wind began to blow. The wind caused the waves to pound against their boat. Jesus told the storm, "Be still!" The storm suddenly stopped, and once again the waves were calm.

Jesus healed people. Once He healed a blind man, and many times He made sick people well. One day, He fed more than 5,000 people with only a small amount of food from a little boy's lunch. But everyone had plenty to eat and there were even leftovers!

Jesus was a friend to everyone. He wanted to do good things for all of His friends and everyone He met. Jesus said, "You are my friends," and "I love you." Jesus was God's Son and He went about doing good things.

Open the Bible, and read: Jesus went about doing good (see Acts 10:38); Jesus said, "You are my friends" (see John 15:14); and Jesus said, "I love you" (see John 15:9).

Say a prayer: Dear God, thank You for Jesus. Thank You for all the good things He did. Help me to do good things so I can be like Jesus. Amen.

ON THE GO

•Spend time reading or listening to Bible stories about the good things Jesus did. Also talk about the miracles that Jesus did. Help your child know that Jesus did things people cannot do. Read these stories:
  —Jesus feeds the 5,000 (see Mark 6:30–44).
  —Jesus heals the blind man (see Mark 8: 22–26).
  —Jesus calms the storm (see Mark 4:35–41).
•Purchase a cassette tape of Bible stories to keep in the car. Listen to other stories about the good things Jesus did as you are on the go. Or make your own tapes. Record yourself reading a Bible story. As you drive along, play the tape while your child looks at his favorite Bible story book.
•Help your child to understand that only Jesus can do miracles.
•Guide your child to think of good things he can do to be like Jesus:

—Visit someone who is sick. Take this person a card, a fruit basket, or a picture your child has drawn. Or make a cassette with your child singing some of his favorite songs about Jesus.

—Help a neighbor who is in need. With your child, run errands for the neighbor. Pick up his newspaper and mail and take it to him.

—Take food to your local food bank. Let you child help collect food items and go with you to make the delivery.

—Guide your child to smile at everyone he sees today.

—Pray with each other.

I Can Be Like Jesus

GROWING

Day 1—God sent His Son, Jesus, into the world so you can know what God is like. All the things Jesus did show you what God is like. Jesus did good things. Jesus did kind things. Jesus helped others. Jesus loved others too. And Jesus loves you. Jesus even loved His enemies.

Did you know that you can be like Jesus? You are like Jesus when you show love to others. What are some ways you show love to others?

You are like Jesus when you help others. Whom can you help? How can you help them?

You can pray for others. Whom do you pray for? What do you pray for? What kinds of things can you tell God?

You can be kind to others. How are you kind to your friends? Your family? Your teachers?

Day 2—Sometimes it is very hard to be like Jesus. You can ask God to help you be more like Jesus every day, and He will. God will help you love people, even those who may act like they don't love you. God will show you ways to help people. He'll give you ideas about how you can be kind. And God will be waiting to talk to you every day as you pray and tell Him what's going on in your life. Every day you can become more and more like Jesus. Isn't it good to know that you can be like Jesus?

Open the Bible, and read: Jesus loves you (see John 15:12); help one another (see Galatians 5:13); pray for one another (see James 5:16); and be kind to one another (see Ephesians 4:32).

Say a prayer: Dear God, help me to be more like Jesus. I want

to treat others with kindness and show them love. I want to help others too. Show me how I can be more like Your Son, Jesus. Amen.

On the Go

- As you take your child to childcare, church, the grocery store, and other places, ask him to think of all the ways he can be like Jesus. Play a game of "I Can Be Like Jesus When . . .". Take turns and include other family members in the game.
- During the evening at home, spend time as a family playing a game of simple charades. Suggest that your child act out a way he is being like Jesus, and ask family members to guess what he is doing. Take turns allowing all family members to act out how they too can be like Jesus.
- When your child does something like Jesus would do, offer sincere praise for his efforts. Say: You are like Jesus. Thank You, God, that Jamie is like Jesus.

Jesus Had Friends

GROWING

Day 1—Jesus had many friends. When Jesus started traveling to many different places to tell people about God, He asked 12 men to go with Him. These 12 men were Jesus' special helpers. They were called disciples. Each one was very different from the others, yet they were alike in some ways too. They all loved Jesus and wanted to follow Him. They followed Jesus everywhere He went. Sometimes they didn't understand everything that Jesus said or did. They still listened and tried to learn. Jesus loved the disciples. They were His friends.

Day 2—The disciples were like any other friends. Sometimes they got angry at each other. Other times they laughed and had fun. They liked to share a good meal and talk about their day. They prayed, read from the Bible, and Jesus taught them even more things about God. Jesus was very kind and patient with the disciples. Jesus was a good friend to the disciples.

Jesus had other friends too. Jesus made friends with a man named Zacchaeus who was a tax collector. Jesus made friends with two sisters named Mary and Martha. And Jesus made friends with little children.

Jesus wants to be your friend. Jesus wants to be your best friend!

Open the Bible, and read: Jesus said, "You are my friends" (see John 15:14).

Say a prayer: Dear God, thank You that Jesus is my best friend. Thank You that He cares for me and loves me. Help me to love Jesus so I can be a good friend to Him too. Amen.

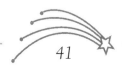

On the Go

•Teach your child to sing the song "My Best Friend Is Jesus" or another song you know about Jesus' love. Talk to your child about his friends. Discuss what makes a person a good friend. Help your child to know that Jesus is his best friend. Sing this song as you are driving in the car, taking a walk, or putting away the dishes.

•Plan a Friendship Party. Encourage your child to invite his friends over. Play games, sing songs, serve snacks, and then tell one of the following Bible stories:

—Jesus Calls the Disciples (Mark 3:13–19 or Luke 6:12–16)

—Zacchaeus (Luke 19:1–10)

—Jesus and the Little Children (Luke 18:15–17)

—Martha and Mary (Luke 10:38–42)

•Lead a group of young children to form a circle, hold hands, and sing this song to the tune of "Ring Around the Roses."

We are all good friends.
We're kind to one another.
Helping, loving.
We're all good friends! (Guide children to fall to the ground.)

The Donkey Ride

GROWING

Day 1—News about Jesus spread everywhere. Everybody was talking about Jesus. "Have you heard about Jesus and what all He does?" they would ask.

"Could Jesus really be sent from God?"

People thought God would send a savior to the world who would be like a great leader in the army. Even Jesus' friends thought this. They found it hard to believe that God's Son would be so kind and loving.

Jesus thought about a lesson He could teach the people. He told two of His helpers to get a donkey for Him to ride into the city of Jerusalem. "You're kidding, right?" asked one of the disciples.

"No, I'm not. I will ride into Jerusalem on a donkey," smiled Jesus.

So Jesus rode the donkey into Jerusalem to show the large crowds of people that He was a very simple man who did not want to be an army leader. He just wanted to show love and peace. The people did not understand. They bowed down and shouted, "Hosanna! Hosanna!" That meant, "Save us now!" They still thought Jesus wanted to be like a great army leader. They did not understand.

Day 2—The leaders of the city heard that Jesus was riding into Jerusalem on a donkey. They heard that the people were bowing down and shouting, "Hosanna! Hosanna!"

They didn't like this at all. The leaders were afraid that Jesus was trying to take over their work in the city. They were afraid that Jesus would rule instead of them. So the leaders started to think of ways they could get rid of Jesus. "We must get Jesus," one leader said. "He is going to take over, and we will no longer be rulers."

The people and the leaders were so wrong. Jesus didn't want to take over. He wasn't trying to show off either. He just wanted the people to know that He was a man who wanted to give everyone in the world peace and love. He wanted them to know about God.

Open the Bible, and read: When Jesus came to the city, everyone was asking "Who is this man?" (see Matthew 21:10).
    For further reading, refer to Matthew 21:1–11. (Note: Read only a short part of this at one sitting as preschoolers have short attention spans.)

Say a prayer: Dear God, help me to know who Jesus is and to do the things that He has taught me in Your Word. Amen.

ON THE GO
•Plan an outing with your family to go to a farm or a petting zoo to see a donkey. Prior to the visit, make arrangements with the owners of the donkey for your preschooler to pet the donkey; feed him; and if possible, with close supervision, ride him. Take a photo of your child with the donkey. On the way back home, remind your child that Jesus chose to ride a donkey to help teach the people about who He was.
•If you can't go to a farm or petting zoo, help your child draw a picture of a donkey. Provide drawing paper, markers, and fabric made of brown fur. Guide your child to cut out pieces of the fabric scraps and glue to his donkey pattern. Underneath write, *Jesus rode a donkey.*

Church Is the Place for Me!

GROWING

Day 1—Jesus' family went to church, and Jesus wants you to go to church too. Why do you think it is important to go to church?

You can learn more about God and His Son, Jesus, when you go to church. You can have fun at church as you learn. You can paint pictures; build with blocks; play games; read the Bible and other good books; sing songs; play musical instruments; make new friends; and hear stories about God, Jesus, and missionaries too.

You can pray at church. You can pray alone or with your friends and teachers. You can also give money when you go to church. The money you give helps many people. You can be a helper at church. You can help your teachers pick up toys and clean up your classroom. You can say thank you to your pastor and the other people who work at your church to help you learn about Jesus. You can learn to worship God at church as you listen to your teachers and your pastor, sing songs, pray, and read the Bible.

Day 2—You can learn about God and Jesus when you meet with other people in a church building. You can also learn about God and Jesus in a church that meets in a neighbor's home, in a school, or in another kind of building. Wherever you meet, you can still learn about God. Your church (no matter what kind of building it has) is a very special place.

People at church learn about God, and then they try to be like Jesus. They want to show their love to God, so they work together to help others. They are kind to others. They also show love to one another. That makes Jesus happy.

Going to church is fun, and it's what God wants you to do.

Open the Bible, and read: I like to go to church (see Psalm 122:1); Jesus went to church (see Luke 4:16); bring an offering to church (see Malachi 3:10); and we work together (see 1 Corinthians 3:9).

Say a prayer: Thank You, God, for my church. Thank You for my pastor and my teachers at church. Thank You for all the people who help me learn more about You. Amen.

ON THE GO

•Take your child to church and Sunday School every Sunday. Be sure to go with him! Get your child involved in preschool choirs and missions classes too.

•If your child has never visited a church, consider taking him to the church before he attends on Sunday. Call ahead of time and ask for a tour. Show your child the room(s) where he'll be in class. Ask if your child can meet the pastor, children's minister, and other leaders.

•Help your child make a church building. He can build a church with his blocks, draw or paint a church building, or decorate a box to look like a church building. He can also use fabric or paper scraps to make a church mosaic. As your child works, talk about the importance of going to church and the many kinds of church buildings in your area.

•When you travel by different kinds of church buildings, point these out to your child. Thank God for all kinds of places where people can come to learn about Him.

Part II

Growing in God's Word

PARENT POINTERS
- Help your child become aware that the Bible is a special book.
- Lead your child to know that the Bible is God's Word, and that God's Word is for him.
- Teach your child that the Bible has two parts, the Old Testament and the New Testament. Guide him to understand that the Bible is made up of many books.
- Suggest your child learn Bible thoughts that lead him to help, love, be kind to, and pray for others.
- Help your child know what Bible thoughts mean.
- Guide your child to know that the Bible has rules. Encourage your child to recognize the Ten Commandments as God's rules.
- Teach your child proper care for the Bible.

The Holy Bible: What a Special Book!

GROWING

The Bible is a very special book. It is special because it tells you about God and His Son, Jesus. Every time you read the Bible or hear a story from the Bible, you learn something about God. That is why we call it the Holy Bible. Holy means "coming from God." And the Bible comes from God.

The Bible tells you what God is like. It also tells you what Jesus is like and how you can be more like Him. The Bible tells you that God loves you so much that He sent His Son, Jesus, to be your best friend. When you read the Bible or hear stories from it, you learn what God wants you to do. All that the Bible says is from God, and you can trust God to help you know the right things to do. God has a plan for your life. As you keep growing, continue to read your Bible. God will help you to know what that plan is.

When you open your Bible to a marked verse, you can learn what that verse means and then you can do what that verse says. That makes God very happy. The Bible—now that's a special book!

Open the Bible, and read: All that the Bible says is from God (see 2 Timothy 3:16).

Say a prayer: Thank You, God, for such a special book, the Holy Bible. Teach me to know more about You as I read and hear stories from the Bible. Help me to be more like Your Son, Jesus. Amen.

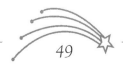

On the Go

- Place all the Bibles in your home in a dish drainer book display. Stand them up in the drainer, and use the utensil compartment to hold bookmarks your child can make from construction paper strips and markers. As your family reads the recommended Bible thoughts in this book, write them on a marker. Place the marker at the appropriate place in the Bible. Place the dish drainer display on a special table or shelf in your house.[1]
- When you are on the go with your child, together sing this tune to "The Farmer in the Dell."

> *My Bible is so special.*
> *My Bible is so special.*
> *It is my favorite book of all.*
> *My Bible is so special.*
>
> *It tells me about God.*
> *It tells me about God.*
> *That God loves me so very much.*
> *He sent His Son, Jesus.*
>
> *I want to be like Jesus.*
> *I want to be like Jesus.*
> *The Bible helps me learn the ways*
> *That I can be like Jesus.*

Parent Pointer

If you have replaced old Bibles at your house with new ones, consider giving the old ones to a homeless or women's shelter, a nursing home, a home for unwed mothers, or a prison ministry.

Yes! God's Word Is for Me!

GROWING

Did you know that the Bible was written for you? It's true.
God's Word was written just for you, your family, and your
friends. God loves you very much and wants you to know
what the Bible teaches.

A long, long time ago God helped some people write the
Bible because He wanted to help everyone know how they
should live and how they should treat others. God told the
people what He wanted in the Bible. They wrote stories,
songs, letters, poems, and rules in the Bible.

As you read the Bible, ask God to help you learn what
His words mean. Open the Bible every day, and learn how
God wants you to live. God's Word is written just for you!
Now say it out loud: Yes! God's Word is for me!

Lead your child to learn the following song. Sing to the
tune of "Bingo."

> The Bible is God's Word for me.
> And tells me what to do.
> God's Word is for me! God's Word is for me! God's Word
>   is for me!
> Yes, God's Word is for me!

Open the Bible, and read: The Bible is useful for teaching us
how to live (see 2 Timothy 3:16).

Say a prayer: Dear God, thank You for giving me the Bible.
Thank You for telling people what to write in the Bible. Help
me to know what the words in the Bible mean and to do
what they say. I'm glad that God's Word is for me! Amen.

ON THE GO

•Take your child shopping to purchase his own Bible or give him one as a gift. Make it a special event as you visit a Christian bookstore and look at different Bibles. Help your child choose a Bible with realistic, colorful illustrations. After the Bible shopping spree, celebrate with Bible cake (see the following recipe) and ice cream.

BIBLE CAKE

Work together as a family to make this recipe. Find the Bible verses in the recipe to discover what you need to make the cake. Mark these verses in your Bible.

4 1/2 cups 1 Kings 4:22 (plain flour)
2 cups Jeremiah 6:20 (sugar)
2 cups Nahum 3:12 (figs)
2 tablespoons 1 Samuel 14:25 (honey)
6 Jeremiah 17:11 (eggs)
1 pinch 2 Chronicles 9:9 (spices such as nutmeg and cinnamon)
1 cup Judges 5:25 (butter)
2 cups 1 Samuel 30:12 (raisins)
2 cups Numbers 17:8 (almonds)
1 pinch Leviticus 2:13 (salt)
1/2 cup Judges 4:19 (milk)

Cream the butter and sugar. Add eggs. Use a mixer on high speed and beat for 5 minutes. Sift flour, salt, and spices. Combine honey and milk. Mix raisins, figs, and almonds together with 1 tablespoon of the flour. Add flour mixture alternatively with milk to the butter mixture. Mix at a low speed. Fold in the fruit. Pour into a loaf pan and bake 50 minutes at 325°F. Allow to cool; then serve warm with ice cream. Yummy!

The Parts of the Bible

GROWING

Day 1—The Bible has two different parts. One part is called the Old Testament. The other part is called the New Testament. That's easy to learn—the Bible has an old part and a new part. The Old Testament tells about God and the world before Jesus was born. God loved us so much, though, that He sent His Son, Jesus. In the New Testament you learn about Jesus and how you can be like Him.

Day 2—Each part of the Bible contains many different books. The Old Testament has different books. The New Testament has many books too. Each of these books has chapters. Each chapter has verses. You can learn many of the verses in these books of the Bible.

Both the Old Testament and the New Testament tell you true stories about people who lived a long time before you and your family. All of these stories help you know how to live your life today.

God wants you to read the Bible. When you get a little older, you will be ready to learn the names of all the different books in the Bible. You can learn what each book is about too.

Open the Bible, and read: The Bible is useful for teaching us how to live (2 Timothy 3:16).

Say a prayer: God, I want to learn more about You as I read the Bible and hear Bible stories. Help me learn what the Bible thoughts mean so I can be more like You. Amen.

ON THE GO

•As a family, look through the Bible together. Point out to your child the different parts of the Bible (the Old and New Testaments). Thumb through the Bible and point out the different books. Then choose one book of the Bible such as Psalms. Point out some of the chapters and verses. Let your child see if he can find the numerals marking the verses.

•As you read the Bible daily with your child, name the book of the Bible from which you are reading. Move your finger from left to right as you point to the words in the verse(s). Say: We are reading a verse from the Book of Psalms. Psalms is a book in the Bible. It is in the Old Testament.

•Make simple Bible puzzles. Provide three pieces of sturdy cardboard. On each piece of cardboard, draw a Bible as large as possible. Divide each piece of cardboard in half by drawing a zigzag line either diagonally, horizontally, or vertically. Cut the cardboard apart on the lines. Lead your child to put the puzzle pieces together. Talk about the Bible having two parts, the Old Testament and the New Testament.

One Another Verses

GROWING

Day 1—Did you know that the Bible has "one another" verses in it? What do you think a "one another" verse is? It is a verse in the Bible that has the words *one another* in it. These words help you remember the special verses. These special verses in the Bible tell you how to treat others. God wants you to love others, help others, pray for others, and be kind to others. Look at these verses, and see if you can say them. Think about the ways you can love, help, pray for, and show kindness to others.

Love one another (see 1 John 4:7).
Help one another (see Galatians 5:13).
Pray for one another (see James 5:16).
Be kind to one another (see Ephesians 4:32).

Day 2—Jesus tells us in the Bible to treat others like we want to be treated. How do you like to be treated? Do you like it when someone is kind to you? Why? Do you like it when someone is mean to you? Why not?

Learn the one another verses. Every day show your friends and family you know what these verses mean. Help someone, love everyone, pray for a friend, and show an act of kindness to someone. When you do what these verses say you should do, you are being like Jesus. Now isn't it exciting to know that one another verses help you become like Jesus?

Open the Bible, and read: Help one another (see Galatians 5:13); love one another (see 1 John 4:7); pray for one another (see James 5:16); and be kind to one another (see Ephesians 4:32).

Say a prayer: Dear God, show me ways that I can help others. Teach me to love others and to be kind to them too. Thank You, God, for my friends, family, and teachers. Amen.

ON THE GO
To help your child learn the "love one another" Bible thoughts:
•Guide him to cut out heart shapes from different colors of construction paper. On each one write the Bible thought, *Love one another (see 1 John 4:7).* Help him use markers, yarn, rickrack, and stickers to decorate the heart cutout. Encourage him to give a heart cutout to friends or family members to let them know he loves them.
•Help your child call a relative who lives in another city to say, "I love you."
•Encourage your child to hug family members every day.

To help your child learn the "pray for one another" Bible thoughts:
•Help your child bake a batch of cookies or pack a fruit basket and take them to your pastor, church staff, or teachers at church. Attach a card that reads *I'm praying for you.* Help your child pray every day for these people.
•Guide your child to make a prayer chain. Think of all the people you can pray for. Write their names on strips of construction paper. Fold the strips and connect them together with tape or glue to make a chain. Help your child hang up the chain in his room and remember to pray for these people each day. Add names to the chain every day.
•Make Bible verse markers, and place them in your Bible marking the "pray for one another" Bible thoughts. Underline these in your Bible. Take time every day to read the Bible. As you ride in the car, pray for the families and people who live in houses, apartments, mobile homes, and retirement or nursing homes that you see. Take walks and pray for your neighbors. Also pray for people you see at

grocery stores, malls, or parks.
•Help your child make get-well cards for children in the hospital. On the cards, write, *I'm praying for you to get well soon!* Take your preschooler with you to make the delivery to the hospital.

To help your child learn the "be kind to one another" Bible thoughts:
•Help your child write each "be kind to one another" thought or verse on a piece of cardstock or poster board. Use markers to draw what the verse means. Or place stickers on the outside to make a border. Cut out magazine pictures of people showing love and kindness and helping each other and glue these to the poster. Display the poster in a place where your child can see it every day.
•Remind your child to say please and thank you when talking with friends and family.

To help your child learn the "help one another" Bible thoughts:
•Lead your child to think of ways he can help family members. Guide him to make a Helping Coupon on a notecard or trace his hand on a piece of paper to make a Helping Hand. Or, ask him to draw a Happy Helper (smiley face) on a white paper plate. On the coupon, hand, or plate write what chore your child can do to help, such as *make my bed, put away the dishes, pick up toys, feed the dog,* or *help work in the yard.* Encourage your child to give this to a parent, grandparent, or sister or brother.
•Sing the "One Another Song" below to the tune of "Row, Row, Row Your Boat:"
> *Help, help, help one another.*
> *Help others today.*
> *Merrily, merrily, merrily, merrily*
> *Help is on the way.*

Love, love, love one another.
Love others today.
Merrily, merrily, merrily, merrily
Love is here to stay.

Pray, pray, pray for one another.
Pray for others today.
Merrily, merrily, merrily, merrily
Pray for others always.

Be kind, kind, kind to one another.
Be kind to others today.
Merrily, merrily, merrily, merrily
Be kind in every way.

The Ten Commandments Are God's Laws

Growing

Day 1—A very long time ago, a man named Moses helped the Hebrew people escape from being slaves. He led the Hebrews into the desert far away from their enemies. Now they were free, and they were so excited to be free that they danced and celebrated. But soon after they arrived in the desert, they became angry with Moses. They were angry because they had run out of water to drink. They also had very little food left.

Moses told the people that God loved them and cared about them and He would meet their needs. It was hard for them to remember that because they were so thirsty and hungry. "If God cares, then why don't we have water to drink and food to eat?" asked one Hebrew man.

The Hebrews seemed to get more and more upset. Moses prayed to God for help. God told Moses to climb up a mountain. Moses told the people to wait for him at the bottom of the mountain, and they did. But as they stood there waiting for Moses to come back down from the mountain, they saw a big billow of smoke rising above it. It was thundering and the earth shook below their feet. The people were so frightened. "Where is Moses? What if he doesn't come back down?"

Day 2—Moses was fine on the mountaintop because God was with him. God told Moses He had a message for the Hebrew people. He wanted to tell them ten important things. These ten important things God told Moses are called the Ten Commandments.

Moses came down from the mountain and told the people about the commandments. The people were happy to

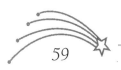

know that God would take care of them if they followed these rules. Soon the people once again had food and water. They praised God and thanked Him for caring about them.

God wants us to do what His rules in the Bible say. You too can learn how to live God's way when you know what these Ten Commandments, or rules, are. Long after God gave people the Ten Commandments, He sent Jesus to show us how to live. The Ten Commandments and Jesus help us live like God wants us to live.

Open the Bible, and read: All that the Bible says is from God (see 2 Timothy 3:16).

Say a prayer: Thank You, God, for giving Moses the Ten Commandments. Help me to learn what these commandments mean so I can live the way You want me to live. Amen.

ON THE GO
•Spend time with your child talking about the importance of rules. As you are going to different places, talk about different traffic signs you see. Talk about how these rules help you to be safe on the streets and roads.
•Before playing a game or taking your child to his preschool class, a movie, a restaurant, or church, talk about the rules at each place. Remind your child why it is important to obey those rules.

The First Commandment:
Love and Obey God

GROWING

The first commandment says that God is God and will take care of His people. It also says that we must love and obey Him and have no other gods.

The Hebrew people didn't know what to do until God gave them the Ten Commandments. They weren't sure how to live their lives, but God made it very clear to them when He gave them the rules, or the Ten Commandments, they were to follow.

This first commandment says that there is only one God. Now God already knows everything about you, but He wants you to know all about Him too. You can learn about God when you read the Bible, pray, and do what the Bible tells you to do. God says, "Obey me and have no other gods." If you do what God wants you to do, God will take care of you at all times. Love God, and obey Him!

Open the Bible, and read: I am God. You should not have any other gods before me (see Exodus 20:2–3).

Say a prayer. Dear God, I want to obey You and follow what You tell me in the Bible. I love You, God. Amen.

ON THE GO

•Use a long piece of paper to make a banner. At the top of the banner help your child write in large letters, *We Love and Obey God!* At the bottom of the banner write, *I am God and I will take care of my people. Love me and obey me and have no other gods (see Exodus 20:2–3).* Spread the banner on the floor. Provide markers, stickers, tempera paints, and different sponge shapes. As a family, draw or paint pictures that show ways your family can love and obey God.

Display the banner in a place where everyone can see it. After you have used the banner at home, donate it to your church for a bulletin board; or give it to a children's home or hospital, a nursing or retirement home, or perhaps to a friend.

•Help your child learn to say the Bible thoughts, *I am God and I will take care of my people. Love me and obey me and have no other gods (see Exodus 20:2–3),* then mark them in your Bible.

The Second Commandment: God Is First!

GROWING

Day 1—The second commandment says that God wants you to make Him the most important thing in your life. Remember the Hebrew people? They stayed in the desert for a very long time and they became very unhappy. But when God gave them the Ten Commandments, they finally understood how much God loved and cared for them. They learned to obey God and do what He said. They learned that they could trust God. They made God the first and most important thing in their lives. Because they learned to obey God, soon it was time for them to leave the desert and go to a new land. There they had lots of food to eat and water to drink. They put God first and God cared for them.

Day 2—Some people who lived at the time of the Hebrews and Moses did not make God first. Instead, they made statues out of wood, gold, or stone. Then they prayed to these statues. They made these statues the most important things in their lives. That made God very sad. You see, God made the earth and everything in it. God loves you and He will always care for you and help you. No statue can do that.

Today some people still do not make God first in their lives. They make other things more important than God. Now think about ways that you can make God first and most important in your life. Talk with your family and friends about what you will do to make God first.

Open the Bible, and read: Make God the most important thing in your life (see Exodus 20:4).

Say a prayer: God, sometimes I make other things more important than You. Please help me to put You first at all

times. Remind me to make You the most important thing always. Help me to trust You. Amen.

ON THE GO

•Lead your preschooler to make two collages. First guide him to look through old magazines and find pictures of things that are important to him. Such pictures may include toys, clothes, computer games, or a pet dog or cat. Ask your child to cut out the pictures and glue them to a piece of poster board or heavy cardstock to make a collage. Say: Sometimes people make these things more important than God. Next, have your child find pictures of people helping others, reading the Bible, praying, or going to church. Encourage your child also to cut out these pictures and glue them to another piece of poster board. Say: When you show love or help others, pray, go to church, and read the Bible, that lets God know that you are putting Him first.

The Third Commandment: Be Careful How You Say God's Name

GROWING

God's name is important. How you say and use God's name is important too. God wants you to use His name when you pray and when you tell others about the good things He does.

At all times God wants you to love Him, so you should be careful about how you say and use God's name. God is very sad if you use or say His name in a way that is disrespectful.

Did you know that God knows all things? Did you know that God can do things that people cannot do? God is greater and smarter than anyone. He is in charge of you and everyone else in the whole wide world. That is why you should never say God's name in a bad way. You can show God your love when you use His name to bring honor to Him. Always be very careful how you speak God's name.

Open the Bible, and read: Be careful how you say God's name (see Exodus 20:7).

Say a prayer: Dear God, You know everything about me. You are wise, great, and loving. I love You, God. Please help me to be careful when I speak Your name. Let the words I say about You bring You great joy! Amen.

ON THE GO

•Lead your preschooler to help you make a name tag necklace for each family member. Provide pieces of sturdy cardboard, markers, hot glue, hole punch, yarn or ribbon, and plastic gemstones. Help your child write each family member's name on a card. Tell your child what his name

means. Tell him why you gave him his name. If you know what other family members' names mean, write the meaning underneath each name. Then hot glue the gemstones to decorate around the edges of the card. (Be careful when using hot glue near a preschooler.) Punch a hole in the top of the card. Loop the ribbon through the hole and tie it to make a necklace. Ask your preschooler to present the name tags to the family. Ask everyone to wear his name tag at dinner. Talk about the importance of each person's name. Remind everyone that his name is important. Say: Your name is important to you. You like it when people say good things about your name, right? God's name is the most important name of all. That is why you should be careful how you say and use God's name.

- Make Name Crackers. You will need 1 cup of flour, 1/8 teaspoon garlic powder, 1/8 teaspoon salt, 4 tablespoons sesame seeds, 4 tablespoons cold water, 5 tablespoons butter, a bowl, mixing spoons, applesauce, and a cookie sheet. Mix the dry ingredients. Then cut the butter in the mixture until it is crumbly. Form into a ball and knead at least 10 times. Roll into a long thin piece, and then shape into letters or names. Flatten on the cookie sheet and bake 15 minutes at 350°F. Serve with the applesauce as you talk about the importance of God's name and your name too.[2]

The Fourth Commandment: Rest on One Special Day Each Week

GROWING

Day 1—God tells you in His fourth commandment that one day each week should be a day of rest. That day has a special name. It is called the Sabbath day. That means you should keep the day holy. Do you remember what the word *holy* means? *Holy* means "coming from God." So there is one special day coming from God that you should keep just for Him. God wants you to spend time on this day learning and thinking about Him.

Day 2—God also wants us to relax and take time to rest on this special day each week. God gives us six days each week to work and play, but on the seventh day, He tells us to rest. Did you know that even God took time to rest after He made the entire world? God made the earth and all that is in it. He made animals, flowers and trees, the oceans and dry land, the stars and moon to shine at night, and the sun to shine during the day. God made everything good, but He wanted to take time to relax so He could enjoy His creation. And that's exactly what God wants you to do too.

Day 3—Busy families like yours may find it hard to keep the fourth commandment. There is always so much to do. It seems like there is so little time. But God says that if you rest and relax on this special Sabbath Day, then you will feel better and have more energy and strength to do the things you need to do on the other days of the week. When you feel rested and relaxed, you'll probably get more done too. So remember to rest one day a week, and keep that day for

God. Thank God for all the good things He has given you to enjoy. Relax! Rest! This is God's fourth law.

Open the Bible, and read: Rest on the Sabbath Day and keep it holy (see Exodus 20:8).

Say a prayer: Thank You, God, for a special day each week to rest. Help me each week to take this special day and make it a day to think about all the good things You give me to enjoy. Amen.

ON THE GO
- Go with your child to church and Sunday School each Sunday to learn more about God.
- Invite friends and neighbors to come to your house for a glass of juice or lemonade. Share a favorite Bible verse with them.
- Spend time talking and telling family stories.
- Listen to Christian music together as a family. Sing familiar songs about God or Jesus to each other.
- Read a Bible story; then ask your child to retell the story in his own words.
- Validate family members by telling each one what you think is so special about him.
- Take a walk with your family. Thank God for good things He has given you to enjoy.
- Pray with your family.
- Take a nap and rest!

The Fifth Commandment: Honor Your Father and Mother

GROWING

God planned for families. God planned for you to have a mother and a father. Your mother and father love you very much. God loves you too. And God loves your mother and father.

God tells you in His fifth commandment that you are to honor your mom and dad. When you honor someone, you show them respect and love. That means you listen to them and do not make fun of them.

Sometimes you may not like the things your mom and dad tell you to do. Other times it may be easy for you to do what they ask you. But God says no matter what your mother and father do or ask you to do, you are to honor them. God wants families to honor and love each other. God loves you and shows His kindness to you. When you love your mom and dad and treat them with kindness, you are obeying God's fifth commandment.

Now think about the things your mom and dad do that make you feel safe and loved. Thank them for loving you. In return, love them too!

Open your Bible, and read: Honor your father and mother (see Exodus 20:12).

Say a prayer: Dear God, I love my mom and dad. Thank You that they care for me and love me. Help me to treat them with kindness. Help me to show them how much I love them. Amen.

ON THE GO

•Give your child a paper plate and crayons. Encourage him
to draw a picture of his mother and father in the center of
the plate. If you prefer, give your child a photo of his mom
and dad and suggest he glue it to the center of the plate.
(Be sensitive if your child lives with only one parent.)
Around the top and bottom edges of the plate, help your
child write the Bible thought *Honor your father and mother
(see Exodus 20:12).* Use a plate stand to prop up the paper
plate in your child's room where he can see it every day. As
your child shows kindness and respect to his parents, thank
him for doing what God's fifth commandment says to do. If
you would like to keep this artwork for many years, purchase and use a plastic plate and paints at a local craft
store. Often the plate and paints come in a kit.

The Sixth Commandment: Do Not Hurt or Kill Another Person

GROWING

Day 1—A long time ago lived two brothers named Cain and Abel. Cain was a farmer and Abel was a shepherd. One day Cain and Abel brought offerings to give to God. Cain had done some bad things and had forgotten about God, but Abel was true to God. God was not happy with Cain's offering because he was not true to God. God told Abel that He was happy with his offering because Abel had obeyed Him.

This made Cain very angry so he decided to kill his brother. Cain thought no one saw him kill his brother, but he was wrong. God saw him. God promised to take care of Cain even though he had killed his brother, but God had to punish Cain for doing the wrong thing. God says that no one is to hurt or kill another person.

Day 2—God gives you life. He gives everyone life. When you are alive, you can have fun with your friends and family. You can go to church to learn more about God. You can help other people and tell them about God and His love. You can laugh and cry. You can work and play. You can eat good food. You can rest and sleep. You can do many things when you are alive. It is good to be alive and enjoy the good things God gives us.

God does not want us to hurt others or to kill others. God wants us to love others and never hurt them in any way. God will take care of you. He will take care of your friends, family, and teachers too. Make sure that what you do and what you say do not hurt others.

Open the Bible, and read: Do not hurt or kill another person (see Exodus 20:13).

For further Bible reading, read Genesis 4:1–12.

Say a prayer: Dear God, help me to love others at all times. Teach me ways that I can show people I care about them. Forgive me when I do things that hurt another person. Amen.

ON THE GO

•Play a game of What Will You Do? Cover a potato chip canister with colorful self-adhesive paper. On the front of the can glue a small piece of white paper over the self-adhesive paper. On it write, *What Will You Do?* Write each of the situations below on a strip of construction paper and place the strips inside the can. Cover the can with the plastic lid until ready for use. Take it along on family trips and play the game with your child while riding in the car, train, bus, or flying in a plane. If you play the game at home, encourage your child to role-play what he would do in each situation.[3] Then talk to your child about the importance of how he treats others. Say: God tells you in the sixth commandment that you should not hurt others.

1. Your friends at school will not let you have your time at the computer station. *What will you do?*
2. Some of the children on the playground are being very mean and rude to a new child who just came to your preschool. *What will you do?*
3. You sister broke your new scooter. *What will you do?*
4. Your teacher made you angry when she asked you to put away the blocks. *What will you do?*
5. You went to a birthday party and some of the children laughed at the sweater you were wearing. *What will you do?*

The Seventh Commandment: Husbands and Wives Should Love Each Other

GROWING

God wants husbands and wives to love each other. Their love for each other is a special love shared just between the two of them. God also wants a husband and wife to trust each other and be true to one another too. God planned for husbands and wives to be special friends. When a husband and wife share a special love, trust each other, and stay true to each other, God will bless their friendship.

Every day God is helping you to learn how to be a true friend and how to be a person that others can trust. One day when you grow up, you might have a husband or a wife. You will want to be true to that person. That person will want to be true to you too. And that will make you and God happy.

Open the Bible, and read: Husbands and wives should love each other (see Exodus 20:14).

Say a prayer: Dear God, I want to be a person whom others trust. I want to always be true and honest. Help me to stay that way when I grow up. Amen.

ON THE GO
- Look through your wedding photo album with your child. Talk to him about your wedding day and what a special day it will always be.
- Have a pretend wedding. Ask your child to help you fill a prop box with dress-up hats and clothes, plastic flowers, scarves, and a small pillow with a ring. Encourage your

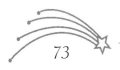

family members all to dress up and pretend they are in the wedding. Let your child choose what role he wants to play.[4]
•If possible, take your child to a wedding; or if he's been to one, ask him to tell what he remembers about it. Tell your child that when a husband and wife get married, they share a very special love.

The Eighth Commandment: Do Not Take Things That Do Not Belong to You

GROWING

God does not want you to take things that do not belong to you. The Bible tells the story of a man named Isaac who lived a long time ago. Isaac was married to Rebekah. They had two sons, Jacob and Esau. The two sons were twins, but Esau was born a few minutes earlier than Jacob. Jacob knew that when Isaac died, Esau would get most of their father's money and rule the family because he had been born first. Jacob was not happy about this so he decided to trick his father.

Now Isaac was getting so old that he could barely see. His eyes were just not working like they used to. He also wasn't able to do some of the things he had always enjoyed doing. He told Esau that if he'd go hunting for him and bring back some meat to make a delicious stew for him, he'd give him (Esau) a special blessing that would make him rich and happy. He would rule over his brother Jacob and all the family. Esau was delighted! So off he went to go hunting.

Rebekah overheard Isaac and Esau talking. She quickly found Jacob who was her favorite son. She told Jacob they needed to hurry and prepare a stew for Isaac before Esau got back with his food. They planned to trick Isaac because they did not want Esau to get the money. Jacob quickly dressed up and pretended he was Esau. He took the stew that Rebekah had prepared and gave it to his father.

His father asked, "Who are you?"

Jacob replied, "I am Esau."

Then Isaac ate the stew and gave Jacob the special blessing. Jacob had taken something that was not his. He took

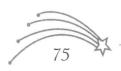

away his brother's right to become head of the family. Once a father gave this special blessing to a son, it could never be taken back.

When Esau returned home and found out what happened, he was very angry with Jacob. Jacob ran away from home to live with his uncle who kept him safe. For a long time Jacob and Esau did not see each other. Many years later, though, God helped them to become friends again.

Open the Bible, and read: Do not take things that do not belong to you (see Exodus 20:15).

Say a prayer: God, You give me everything I need. When I see things that do not belong to me and I want them for myself, help me to trust You to meet all my needs. Amen.

ON THE GO
•Make a Good Deeds chart. When your child returns a book or toy that belongs to someone else, praise him for his honest act. On the chart write, *Jamie returned Jessica's book. Matthew took Steven's toy back.* Celebrate the good deeds that each family member does.[5]

PARENT POINTER
Keep in mind that most preschoolers are not intentionally dishonest. They just perceive things differently than adults do. Help your young child begin to understand this commandment by modeling honesty in your actions every day. For instance, if you have borrowed something from someone, return it, and let your child see you do so.

The Ninth Commandment: Always Tell the Truth

GROWING

Sometimes telling the truth can be scary. You might think you'll get in trouble if you tell the truth about some things. Sometimes you might tell things that are not exactly like they happened to make people like you. Other times you might not know what is real and what is not, so that can make it hard to tell the truth.

It is always best to tell the truth about everything. If you are not sure what is real and what is not, your family and teachers can help you learn the difference. Before long you will understand.

Do you like to pretend? It's fun to pretend when you are playing with your friends, isn't it? You can imagine all kinds of things and have fun with your friends and family. There is a time to pretend and a time to tell the truth.

God tells you in His ninth rule, or law, that you should always tell the truth. When you tell the truth, people will trust you and know that you are a good friend to them.

Open the Bible, and read: Always tell the truth (see Exodus 20:16).

Say a prayer: Dear God, help me know the difference in what is real and what is not. I want to be able to tell the truth so I can keep Your law and be a friend to others. Amen.

ON THE GO

•Join your child in pretend play while he plays with blocks and toy animals, as he dresses up, or while he is watching a cartoon. Let the toy animals "talk" to each other. Laugh together as you watch the cartoon. As you play, ask your

child, "Could this toy pig really talk?" or "Could that dog on the cartoon really drive a car?"

•Lead your child to understand the difference between what is fact and what is fantasy. Make a spinner game. Use a square piece of heavy cardstock or poster board and divide it into six sections. In each section write one of the statements below or write your own ideas. Use a brad to attach a spinner to the center of your board. Lead your child to spin the arrow. When the arrow stops, read the statement on the section of the poster board. Ask your child to tell if the statement is true or not true. (Note: Instead of a spinner, you can give your child large buttons or beanbags to toss onto one of the sections of the game.)

    1. God wants you to tell the truth.
    2. Cats and dogs can talk to each other.
    3. You can fly like a bird.
    4. The Bible is a true book.
    5. Ducks can swim in a pond.
    6. Your toys dance in your room at night.

The Tenth Commandment: Do Not Want Things That Other People Have

GROWING

Day 1—Once there was a boy named Joseph. His father Jacob was very proud of him. To show him how much he loved him, Jacob gave Joseph a beautiful coat made of many different colors. It was red and green and yellow and blue and purple. Never had Joseph seen such a handsome coat!

But Joseph's brothers were very upset that their father had given Joseph the fancy coat. Their father had given them coats too, but nothing as nice as the coat he gave Joseph. They wanted Joseph's coat. The brothers were very jealous of Joseph.

The brothers were also angry with Joseph because he had dreams and he would tell his brothers that some day he would rule over them. Naturally they didn't like Joseph showing off and telling about his dreams. So they started to make fun of Joseph and laugh at him when he told about his dreams. "Dreamer boy, dreamer boy," they'd tease and call out to him. Joseph tried not to let this bother him. He knew that his brothers were jealous.

Day 2—One day Joseph was wearing his beautiful coat when his brothers started to make fun of him again. One of the brothers wanted to kill him, but the oldest brother said it would be better if they just threw him into a deep hole and got rid of him. So they tore off Joseph's coat and they threw Joseph into a hole. Just then the brothers saw some rich men coming towards them. They decided to sell Joseph to these men. Joseph became their slave. The brothers didn't want their father to know what they had done, so they killed a

79

goat. The brothers put the coat in the blood from the goat. They took the coat back to their father and said, "Look what we have. It looks like a wild animal killed Joseph."

Jacob was very sad. He thought Joseph was dead. For many years Joseph did not see his brothers and father again. But later God sent Joseph back to his family, and with God's help they all loved each other again.

God wants you to be happy with the things you have. Thank God for the things you have, and do not want the things that belong to other people.

Open the Bible, and read: Do not want things that do not belong to you (see Exodus 20:17).

For more Bible reading, share the story of Joseph (Genesis 37:12–36).

Say a prayer: Dear God, thank You for all the things you have given me. Help me to be happy with what I have and not to want things that do not belong to me. Amen.

ON THE GO

•Play a game of Yours and Mine with your family. Ask each family member to gather three or four of his most prized possessions and put them all in a box or a large shopping bag. Ask each family member to take out one item at a time. Ask, and say: Whose is this? Yes, Teresa, that is your favorite doll. And this is my favorite book. The doll is *yours* and the book is *mine.*

•Talk to your child about not wanting things that belong to others. Encourage your child to be happy with the things he has.

PARENT POINTER

Remind your child that he and his friends can share their things with each other, but they must return things that do not belong to them.

Take Care of God's Word

GROWING

You have learned that the Bible is a very special book. Your Bible is the most important book that you own. God wants you to take care of the Bible since it is a book about Him. Because the Bible is about God, you and your family should show respect and great care of this special book.

Can you easily find your Bible? If not, put it somewhere in your house right out in the open. Keep magazines, newspapers, food, drinks, and dust off your Bible.

Hold your Bible very carefully. Turn the pages slowly to avoid tearing them. Look at your Bible every day. Ask a parent, other family member, or teacher to read the Bible to you. Choose a good time each day to have Bible time with your family.

Open the Bible, and read: The Bible is useful for teaching us how to live (see 2 Timothy 3:16).

Say a prayer: God, thank You for the Bible. Help me to remember that it is a special book that I should take care of. Amen.

ON THE GO

•As a family, make a special area in your home to keep your Bibles. Clean off an end table, coffee table, or bookshelf. Lay a special tablecloth or covering on the table or shelf. Wipe off Bibles that are dusty and place them on the table or shelf. Around the Bibles, place special Bible bookmarks that your child can use to mark a verse he is learning.
•Model how to care for the Bible, and make sure your child sees you.

Part III
Growing in Family Matters

PARENT POINTERS
• Help your child to know that God planned for families.
• Guide your child to understand that families help each other.
• Lead your child to be aware that a family works together.
• Encourage your child to do his part to help your family.
• Establish family rules.
• Teach your child that there are all kinds of families and that God loves them all.
• Guide your child to know what adoption means.
• Help your child to know that family members may live in different places, but they are still a family.
• Plan family worship.
• Make time for family fun.
• Find time to relax, rest, and slow down. Spend quiet times with God.

God Planned for Families

GROWING

From the very beginning of time, God wanted people to love each other and be a part of a family. Remember the very first man, named Adam? God gave Adam a wife and then they had two sons. They were the first family.

Jesus had a family too. Jesus' mother and father loved Him very much. Jesus' family went to church. They read the Bible together and helped Jesus learn more about God. They worked together and helped each other. They prayed together. God planned for Jesus to have a family.

Open your Bible with someone in your family, and together learn how God planned for Bible families. After you read a story (see suggestions below), talk about how the family in the story learned about God and how they showed their love to God.

God planned for you to have a family too. God loves your family, and He wants your family to love Him. Your family can show that they love God when they help and love each other. Pray together and show kindness to one another.

Open the Bible, and read: Love each other (see John 15:17), and be kind to each other (see Ephesians 4:32).

Some Bible stories about families include:

    Abraham and Sarah—Genesis 17–18; 19; 21:1–7

    Rebekah and Isaac—Genesis 24–25

    Samuel and his family—1 Samuel 1–2

    Joseph and his brothers—Genesis 42–43

(Note: These passages are very long, so read only a small segment daily. Before you start reading a new segment, be sure to review the previous reading with your child.)

Say a prayer: Dear God, I love You. I'm glad You planned for families. Thank You for giving me a family. Thank You for each member of my family. Help me to show my family how much I love them. Amen.

On the Go

•Purchase a plastic photo cube. Insert family photos on each side of the cube. Before eating a meal, reading a devotional, watching your favorite television program, or while listening to music as a family, ask your child to roll the cube gently. Talk about the photo on top of the cube and what your family is doing in it. Ask your child to tell how your family shows their love to God. Say a prayer for your family. After talking about the photo, replace it with another one. Keep the photo cube in a prominent place in your home and refer to at least once a day.

•Look through family photo albums, and talk about special times together as a family.

Families Help Each Other

GROWING

Once there were two cousins. Their names were Mary and
Elizabeth. Mary was married to Joseph. Elizabeth was married to Zechariah. Mary and Elizabeth were both going to
have babies. Mary wanted to go visit Elizabeth so she could
help her. You see, Elizabeth was quite old and wasn't able to
get around very well since she was going to have a baby.
Mary was very young, and she had more energy. She knew
she could be a helper to her cousin Elizabeth.

When Mary arrived at the home of Elizabeth and
Zechariah, they were so glad to see her. Mary stayed for
about three months. Mary helped wash clothes, cook and
clean, and do many other chores. The two women also liked
spending time talking. They talked about their babies. They
laughed together and sang songs about how wonderful God
is. They were glad that they were a family. Mary was glad
that she could help Elizabeth. But the time came for Mary to
leave so she could go back to her husband.

Soon Mary and Joseph had their baby boy. They named
Him Jesus. Elizabeth and Zechariah had their baby too. His
name was John. Jesus and John were cousins. They grew up
to be good friends. They loved each other and always helped
each other too. Families help each other.

Open the Bible, and read: Help one another (see Galatians
5:13).

For further reading, read Luke 1:5–25,39–80.

Say a prayer: Thank You, God, for my family. Thank You that
my family helps me. Show me ways that I can help my
family every day. Amen.

ON THE GO

•Make I Can Help cards. Provide index cards, hole punch, and a plastic or metal ring. Talk to your child about the things he can do at home to help the family. Print each of these ideas on an index card. On the back of each card, suggest your child illustrate a way he can help. Punch a hole in the upper left corner of each card. Attach the cards using the ring. Place the cards in a convenient place to help remind your child how he can help his family. Continue to add more cards as your child thinks of more ways he can help.

Working Together

GROWING

God wants families to work together. Once there was a man named Noah. Noah and his family loved God and wanted to please God. God told Noah and his family to build a boat, a very big boat called an ark. God said, "Build this boat big enough that it can hold two of every kind of animal in the world."

So Noah and his family worked together to build the boat. They worked day and night and night and day. Some of Noah's friends would come by and see Noah's family building the big boat. They made fun of Noah and his family. "Why are you doing this? There's not even any water nearby. You're just being silly," they'd scoff.

But Noah and his family kept working. They worked together for a very long time, and finally one day they finished the boat. Even though people made fun of them and didn't understand what they were doing, Noah's family obeyed God.

Open your Bible, and read: We work together (see 1 Corinthians 3:9).

For further reading this week, read Genesis 6:1 to 9:17.

Say a prayer: Dear God, help my family to do what pleases You. Help us to work together to help each other at all times. Amen.

ON THE GO

•Think of ways your family can work together to get a job done:

   1. Clean off the table together, or prepare dinner or a snack.

2. Play a game.
3. Put away the toys and help clean the house.
4. Roll a ball back and forth.
5. Play on a seesaw as you talk about working together and what *cooperation* means.
6. Place a round tablecloth on the floor. Put a soft ball in the center of the cloth. Have family members work together to lift up the cloth as they hold it around the edges. Work together to toss the ball into the air and catch it in the tablecloth.

•Talk about ways your family can work together to please God. Pray together, read the Bible together, sing praises to God, and help needy families in your community.

Doing My Part

GROWING

Day 1—No one is exactly the same, not even people in a family. Everyone in the family is different. How are you different from others in your family? How are you alike? Even though you are different in some ways, you are alike too. Each person in a family can do his part to help, and that will help make your home a happy place.

Did you know that each person in your family has a part in helping to make your home a happy place? Your mom and dad have a part. Your sisters and brothers have a part. And you have a part too!

Day 2—Your body has many different parts and each part does something special. Your eyes see for you. Your ears hear for you. Your nose smells for you. Your mouth tastes for you. Each body part does something different.

Everyone in your family has a part. When everyone in your family (and that means you too) does his or her part, it helps make your home a happy place. What is your part in your family? What tasks can you do to help your family?

Day 3—Everyone in your church has a part too. Some people in your church teach. Some people sing. Some people play musical instruments. Some people prepare food. Some people preach. People who go to church together do their parts to make church a happy place. You can do your part at church too.

Open the Bible, and read: We are helpers (see 2 Corinthians 1:24), and we work together (see 1 Corinthians 3:9).

For further reading this week, read Luke 10:38–42.

Say a prayer: Dear God, thank You for giving me a family to love. I want to do my part to help my family. Thank You for giving me a church family too. Help me to do my part at church too. Amen.

On the Go

• Talk about the different tasks each family member has. As you do different things around the house, talk about your child's part in helping and how his part helps the family. Offer sincere praise when your child does a task that helps the family.

• Provide a simple puzzle for the family to put together. Give each person in the family several pieces of the puzzle. Put each person's puzzle pieces into a separate resealable plastic bag until ready to use. As you work the puzzle, talk about the importance of each person doing his part to make the puzzle complete.

• If your child plays on a team, talk to him about each person on the team doing his part to help the team.

• As you travel around your community, talk with your child about the parts of your community. When you pass the hospital, police or fire department, a church, or a school, talk about how each place has a part in the community.

• Invite other families to come to your home for a Friendship Salad. Suggest that each family bring a cooked fruit or vegetable. When everyone arrives, work together to decide what ingredients will work best together to make one or more Friendship Salads.[1]

My Family Rules

GROWING

Day 1—Every family has rules. Rules help you know how to behave. Rules remind you to help others, work together, and do your part. Rules help everyone in the family know what they should do and what they shouldn't do.

You can cooperate with your family. That means you work together to get along. You can share with your family. When you have a toy and your brother wants to play with it, you can let him. You can help. You can put away toys, help set the table, look at a picture book with your baby sister, take turns playing a game, or say please and thank you.

God wants you to live happily with each other. He wants you to get along with everyone. Rules can help you to do that. Your family's rules help everyone know what to do.

Day 2—You can accept and obey your family's rules. What are some of the rules in your family? How do you obey those rules? Do you remember learning about the Ten Commandments? Those are laws, or rules, that God gave to His people so they would know how to please Him. When you follow those rules, it makes God happy. When you obey the rules that your family has, it makes your family happy too. Work together to follow God's rules and your family's rules too.

Open the Bible, and read: We work together (see 2 Corinthians 1:24), and obey all His rules (see Deuteronomy 6:2).
For further reading, read Luke 15:1–2,11–32.

Say a prayer: Dear God, I want to make You happy and work together to make my family happy too. Help me to accept and obey Your rules and my family's rules too. Amen.

On the Go

•Call a family meeting to make a chart entitled "My Family Rules." Spend time thinking of three or four rules for your family. State each rule in a positive way and write each on the chart. Provide markers, and lead your child to illustrate each rule. Punch two holes at the top of the chart. Loop a 36-inch length of yarn or string through the holes and tie it. Hang the chart where your family will see it every day. Remind your child about the importance of keeping the rules. Add new rules when appropriate.

Parent Pointer

Be patient with preschoolers when teaching them about rules. Repeat rules often and avoid threats, bribes, and criticisms. Keep in mind that punishment does not teach. Instead choose to discipline to help foster confidence.

All Kinds of Families

GROWING

Day 1—There are all kinds of families. There are families with just a husband and a wife. There are families with a mom and her children. There are families with a dad and his children. And there are families with a mom and dad and their children. There are some children who live with their grandparents or maybe their aunts or uncles and cousins. All of these are families, and God loves them all!

Who is in your family? Who are the people in your friends' families? Some families are like yours. Some families are different from yours. All families are alike in one way, because God loves them. They might be different because they have different people in the family. Or they might like to do different things. No matter who is in your family and what your family likes to do, God loves your family. He will love them always.

Day 2—A long time ago, a woman named Naomi lived in Bethlehem with her husband and their two sons. They liked living in Bethlehem, but one year something very bad happened there. The rains stopped and all the vegetables and fruits could not grow. There was not enough food for all of the people in Bethlehem. Naomi's husband said they should leave Bethlehem and go to a place called Moab. There would be plenty of food to eat there. So Naomi's family traveled a long way and moved to Moab.

The people in Moab were very kind to Naomi's family. They had lots of good food to eat, and they thanked God for it.

Day 3—Naomi's sons soon grew up and got married in Moab. One married a woman named Ruth, and the other married a woman named Orpah. Naomi said, "Ruth and Orpah are just like daughters to me."

Naomi's family was happy, and each person in the family worked together to help the others. Then something very sad happened again. Naomi's husband died. Not long afterwards, her two sons died too. Naomi, Ruth, and Orpah were very sad. They cried and cried. They worried too that they might not have enough money to buy food and would have no place to live since their husbands had died.

Finally Naomi told Ruth and Orpah that she would have to go back and live with her family in Bethlehem. They could take care of her and would not let her starve. She told Orpah and Ruth that they too should go back and live with their families too. Orpah did that. She left and went back to her family, but Ruth did not. "I cannot leave you. I will go wherever you go," said Ruth. "You are my family."

Day 4—Naomi thanked God for Ruth. Naomi and Ruth were family even though both of their husbands had died. Together they traveled back to Bethlehem. They stayed with Naomi's cousin, Boaz. Boaz knew that Ruth had been a helper to Naomi and stayed to help her in Moab.

Boaz fell in love with Ruth. Soon they were married. They had a little boy named Obed. This made Naomi very happy. She was a grandmother. Naomi, Boaz, Ruth, and Obed were now one big happy family.

Open the Bible, and read: Love one another (see 1 John 4:7).
For further Bible reading, read the Book of Ruth.

Say a prayer: Thank You, God, for the people in my family. Thank You for all kinds of families. Thank You for loving them all. Amen.

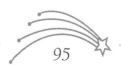

On the Go

•Help your child learn about all kinds of families. Focus on different kinds of families who might live in your neighborhood or community. Invite these families to come to your house for Family Fun. This might be a cookout, a pool party, or something as simple as serving refreshments and getting to know each other. Guide your child to help you make the invitations to send to these families. Ask each family to introduce themselves. Get to know each other and thank God for all kinds of families.

•As you meet different kinds of families in your church, your child's preschool or kindergarten, or in your neighborhood, teach your child to love them. Take a gift basket with a card attached that reads: *We are glad to have your family as new friends. Love one another (see 1 John 4:7).*

•Help your child find four magazine pictures showing four different kinds of families. Cut a piece of poster board into a circle shape, and divide it into fourths, using a marker. Suggest that your child cut out the family pictures and mount each onto a section of the circle. Cut another piece of poster board into a circle that is the same size as the first circle. Cut a section (one-fourth) out of this circle. Place it on top of the picture circle. Punch a hole in the center of both circles. Attach the circles by putting a large brad through both holes. As your child turns the "wheel" and discovers a picture, talk about the kind of family he sees. Thank God for all kinds of families.

What Does Adoption Mean?

GROWING

Day 1—*Adoption!* What a big word! Can you say it? *Adoption.* Think about a baby. Where do babies come from? Does a baby come from the mailman? No, that is silly. Does a baby come from the grocery store? No, that is silly too. You know that a baby comes from a mother and a father who love each other very much. At one time you were a baby too. Your mother and father gave you the gift of life. That is something that no one else can give you. But sometimes a baby or child does not stay with the mother and father who gave it life. The baby or child goes to live with another family. Why would that happen?

There are many reasons. Perhaps the birthparents (the ones who gave the baby its life) were very young and could not take care of the baby. They probably still had a lot of growing up to do. Or maybe the birthparents died. Although that would be very sad, God sent another mother and father to take care of the baby. They wanted to love the baby and care for the baby and make the baby very happy. That is adoption.

Day 2—Families with adopted children are *real* families. The children in adopted families cannot be given back just because they are naughty. Do you know why? Because adoption is forever. Adoptive families will always love and care for their children just as any parents in other families do.

Do you know someone who is adopted? Did they tell you about it? It's good to talk about being adopted. If someone is adopted, their mom and dad probably have told them about it because they want to be honest with their children. God wants us to be honest too. Being honest about adoption makes God happy.

Adoption. It's a big word with a big meaning—being part of a family! And that's just what God planned for us all.

Open the Bible, and read: Love your father and mother (see Exodus 20:12), and love one another (see 1 John 4:7).

Say a prayer: Dear God, thank You for moms and dads who adopt children of all ages. Help adopted children to know how much they are loved by their parents and You. Please take care of all the children who still need to be adopted. Give them moms and dads to love and help them. Amen.

ON THE GO

•Every child (whether adopted or not) needs to know he is special, wanted, and loved. Plan a special family dinner, but keep the guest list a secret. Prior to the dinner, ask your child to help you make several crowns using construction paper, glue, glitter, and markers. Be sure that each child in the family has a crown for himself. Ask your child to help you set the table using a tablecloth, flowers, candles, and your best dinnerware. Encourage your child to dress up in his best clothes right before serving the meal. When he comes to the table, place a crown on each child, and say: You are our special dinner guests tonight. You are like royalty to us, kings and queens. During dinner refer to each child as King Matthew or Queen Danielle. Be sure to say a special blessing for each child before enjoying the meal.[2]

PARENT POINTER

A wonderful picture book about adoption is *I Love You Like Crazy Cakes* by Rose Lewis.

Where Do Families Live?

GROWING

Day 1—Some families do not all live together in the same house. Sometimes a mom and a dad may decide that they can no longer live together. The mom or the dad may move out of the house. Even though the mom or the dad moves out of the house, they are still a mom and dad. Nothing can change that! If a mom or dad moves out of the house and the family no longer lives together, that doesn't mean that the parents don't still love their children. They do love them, and they love them very, very much! Nothing can change that either!

Day 2—When children grow up, they may move out of the house where they have lived with their parents. They may go to college. They may get married and move to a different house. They may get a job and move to a new city to work. Even though moms and dads and their children may all live in different places, they are still a family.

Sometimes aunts, uncles, cousins, or grandparents may come to live with you and your family. That can be a full house, can't it? Sometimes people who might not be related to you at all could live at your house. They would be a part of your family too. All of these people work together to help each other. They love each other too.

Family members can live in different places, but they are still a family. No matter where they live, God loves them all the same.

Open the Bible, and read: Love one another (see 1 John 4:7).

Say a prayer: Thank You, God, for all the people in my family. Thank You for those who live with us and for those

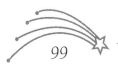

who live away from us. No matter where we live, help us to work together and help each other. Always remind us to show our love to each other. Amen.

ON THE GO

•Cut a house shape from a piece of construction paper. Give your child drawing paper and markers, and ask him to draw all the people who live in your house. Lead him to color, cut out, and glue the family figures to the house shape. Label each figure as Aunt Lucy, Uncle James, etc. At the bottom of the house write, *Look who lives in our house. Love one another (see 1 John 4:7).*

•Show your child pictures of family members who do not live in your house. Lead your child to draw pictures of these family members. Label these drawings with the names of each family member. At the bottom of the drawings write, *Pray for one another (see James 5:16).* Display the drawings so your child will see them each day. Every day pray for the people in your family.

Family Worship

GROWING

Day 1—Worship means to honor God and to show His love to others. God wants your family to show love and honor to Him—to worship Him.

Your family can worship God when you go to church together. At church your family can learn more about God. At church your family can sing songs to praise God. You can hear stories from the Bible. Your family can make new friends who also love God.

Your family can also worship God at home. When your family reads the Bible, sings songs to God, prays together, helps each other, and shows love to other people, you are worshiping God.

Your family can show love and honor to God when you pray together. Your family can pray together anytime, any-where. What can your family pray about? Your family can praise God for all His goodness. Your family can thank God for what He has done. You can ask God to help you with problems. Your family can ask God to help you make good choices. Your family can tell God how you are feeling about things whether they are things that make you happy or sad. Your family members can ask God to forgive them when they don't do the right thing. God hears your family's prayers. God is happy when your family prays together.

Day 2—Families worship God in different ways. Some fami-lies kneel and pray while others may hold hands as they pray together. Some families raise their hands and shout to praise God while some choose to sit and be very calm and quiet. It doesn't matter how your family worships God. The important thing is that you worship together.

You can be a part of your family's worship time. Your family can say Bible verses and talk about what they mean. Your family can pray. Your family can save your money and give it to your church. You and your family can do things to help others. You can obey your parents and do what they say. You can tell others about God and how much He loves them. You can sing songs about God. Your family can find many ways to worship God.

When your family tries to be like Jesus, that honors God. God is pleased when your family worships Him. Praise God! Love God! Worship God!

Open the Bible, and read: Sing praises to God (see Psalm 47:6); I thank God (see 2 Timothy 1:3); I like to go to church (see Psalm 122:1); and give thanks to the Lord for He is good (see Psalm 107:1).

Say a prayer: Dear God, I love You! My family loves You too. You are an awesome God. You are a mighty God. We praise You. Thank You for being so good to us. Help us to be more like Your Son, Jesus. Amen.

ON THE GO

- Worship together as a family. Family worship can include prayer, reading the Bible, and either a devotional thought, object lesson, song, Bible story, or drama (a short play, a puppet show, a choral reading, etc). You might choose to worship before or even during a mealtime; before going to bed, to school, to work; while riding in the car or taking walks; or during a snack time.
- Try something fun. Sit in the middle of your child's bed and worship in your pajamas. During winter, gather around the fireplace and serve hot chocolate while you worship. In warmer weather, take cushions and sit on your patio or deck as you worship. Worship while enjoying a family picnic. Take a Bible, Bible story book, *Growing on the Go*, and

hymnals or recordings about God and Jesus. Make sure your preschooler has a part in family worship.

•Look up the following Bible references to learn about different motions and gestures that people sometimes use when they worship God. Ask family members to do the motions and then choose one of the motions they'd like to use when they worship God.

1. Clap your hands (Psalm 47:1).
2. Fall on your face (Numbers 16:22).
3. Stand (1 Kings 8:22).
4. Bow (Revelation 19:4; Ephesians 3:14).
5. Kneel (Psalm 95:6; Luke 22:41).
6. Dance (2 Samuel 6:14).
7. Lift your hands (Psalm 28:2; 63:4; 1 Timothy 2:8).[3]

Family Fun

GROWING

Your family can have fun together. Your family can have fun in many ways. Your family might like to go on picnics or go camping together. You might enjoy spending time reading together or watching a television program or video. Some families enjoy playing board games or computer games while other families like to go to sporting events such as baseball or football games, fishing, swimming, or ice-skating. Some families sing together and play musical instruments. Other families like to ride their bicycles, and still others like to take hikes. All of these are ways for families to have fun.

God wants your family to spend time with each other and some of that time can be spent having fun. How does your family have fun? Every day do something fun together as a family. Family fun can help families relax and understand each other better. Laugh together as a family and enjoy each other. Have some fun!

Open the Bible, and read: We work (and play) together (see 1 Corinthians 3:9).

Say a prayer: Dear God, help my family to make time for fun and enjoy doing things with each other. Thank You for my family and for fun times with them. Amen.

ON THE GO

• Do simple chores around the house. Teach your child this simple song, sung to the tune of "Are You Sleeping," as he helps you clean up around the house. Continue singing, substituting other chores that your child can help you do.

Who's my helper?
Who's my helper?
Mark helps me.
Mark helps me.
Mark helps me clean up.
Mark helps me clean up.
Thank you, Mark. Thank you, Mark.

- Have fun while riding in the car. Play musical tapes. Enjoy singing along. Find an appropriate book on tape that your child will enjoy listening to while taking a trip. Play counting games or I Spy focusing on different colors. Provide activity bags filled with markers or colored pencils, drawing paper, stickers, picture books, or simple activity books. Don't forget to have some favorite snacks too.
- Have a Family Fun night at least one night a week. Do something special such as play games, try family karaoke, eat something new, order pizza or have a cookout (don't forget to roast marshmallows), spend the night in a tent (in your backyard or in your very own living room), or have a talent show. Reserve this night just for your family. Have fun!
- Take a family vacation. Do something that everyone in your family will enjoy such as camping, fishing, hiking, riding bikes, sledding, or swimming.

Busy, Busy Families

GROWING

Day 1—When your family rushes around and hurries to do things, you might feel tired and cranky. You may whine or start to cry because you feel so rushed. Did you know most young children your age feel the same way when their families rush them too? They are like you. They like to take their time and not rush so much.

Sometimes you can help your family so they aren't so rushed. To help your mom and dad, you may need to lay out the clothes you will wear the next day the night before. You can help your mom make your lunch for school the night before too. Or maybe you and your family need to get up earlier to start the day.

Once there was a woman named Martha who loved to cook. She lived with her sister, Mary, and their brother, Lazarus. Martha was always busy helping people. She liked helping Jesus too. She knew that Jesus often got very tired from all of His work, so she'd invite Him to come to their house and eat a special meal. One evening while Jesus and some other guests were visiting, Martha was busily working getting everything ready for the dinner she was preparing. Martha was also getting angry. She couldn't understand why Mary would not come and help her prepare the meal. She had worked and worked and was getting very tired. *Where was Mary?* she thought.

When Martha went into the sitting area where her guests had gathered, there was her sister. Mary was just sitting at the feet of Jesus. They were talking and laughing and really having a good time. This made Martha even angrier. "Don't you care about me?" she asked. "I'm busy in the kitchen working all alone."

Jesus said, "Oh Martha, please come and sit with us.

Let's all talk. You must come and visit with us first. Then we can all enjoy the special meal you have prepared."

Day 2—Martha smiled. They all sat together and talked about God's love. Jesus helped Martha learn that the most important thing was to spend time with each other. Jesus wanted Martha to spend time with Him like Mary was doing.

Jesus wants your family to spend time with Him too. You can do that by reading your Bibles together, praying, and helping others. Sometimes you may have planned too much to do in one day and not have enough time to spend with Jesus. Has that ever happened?

What are some of the things that keep you busy during the day? Could some of those things wait? Busy families need Jesus! Think about ways your busy family could spend more time with Jesus.

Open the Bible, and read: Jesus said, "You are my friends" (see John 15:14).

Say a prayer: Dear God, help my family to slow down. Help us to find more time to spend with You and to be more like Jesus. Amen.

ON THE GO

- As a family, make every effort to start each day spending time in prayer and Bible reading. Get up a few minutes earlier and gather around the breakfast table to have a family devotional time. If early mornings are impossible, have a devotional time before bedtime.
- As a parent commit to Deuteronomy 6:7–9: "Teach them [God's commands] to your children, and talk about them when you sit at home, and walk along the road. When you lie down, and when you get up. Write them down, and tie them on your hands as a sign. Tie them on your forehead

to remind you, and write them on your doors and gates." Print this verse on a large piece of poster board. Read it to your preschooler and ask him to decorate the poster. Then laminate the poster and put it over a doorway in your home.

•Spend quiet time together. Make a Quiet Corner in your house where your child can escape the hustle and bustle. Cut the top and one side out of a large cardboard box. Guide your child to decorate the box inside and out. Put several cushions and your child's favorite books and a Bible inside the box.

•Help your child learn this fingerplay to help calm him.

> **Sleepy Fingers**
> My fingers are so sleepy; it's time they went to bed.
> So first you, Baby Finger, tuck in your little head.
> Ring Man, now it's your turn, and come, Tall Man great.
> Now Pointer Finger hurry, because it's getting late.
> Let's see if all are snuggled—
> No, here's one more to come.
> So come, lie close, little brother,
> Make room for Master Thumb.
> *(Point to each finger as it is mentioned.)*[4]

•Blowing bubbles can also be a relaxing activity to do with young children. You can make your own bubble solution by mixing two tablespoons of dishwashing liquid with two tablespoons of glycerin (sold in drugstores). Or, purchase ready-made bubbles. You can easily make bubble wands from a six-pack plastic drink holder or a wire coat hanger. Shape the hanger into a wand by pulling the bottom wire until a diamond shape forms. Take the handle of the hanger and twist it tightly. Cover it with masking or duct tape for added protection. As you have fun blowing bubbles, talk about how the light from the sun is broken into different colors to cause the rainbow in the bubbles. Thank God for good things to enjoy.[5]

Part IV

Growing to Be Me

PARENT POINTERS
- Lead your child to discover that he is wonderfully made.
- Help your child learn how to take care of his body.
- Discover how young children learn. Help your child learn as you provide opportunities that are age and developmentally appropriate.
- Point out the many things your child can do. Offer sincere praise for his efforts.
- Guide your child to make good choices.
- Begin showing your child ways he can share with others.
- Help your child to know that he can be honest.
- Teach your child about the importance of giving.
- Talk to your child about making good friends.
- Encourage your child to have friendships with older adults (grandfriends).
- Lead your child to know that he can practice self-control.
- Talk about feelings with your child. Help him find appropriate ways to deal with his feelings.
- Help your child learn to cope with separation anxiety.
- Suggest ways your child can learn to cooperate and work with others. Help your child learn ways to get along with others.
- Lead your child to be aware that God will forgive him when he does wrong. Teach your child to forgive others.
- Guide your child to be patient.
- Talk to your child about his habits. Encourage him to keep good habits; and work together as family to discover what might be creating stress in your child's life, causing harmful habits.
- Guide your child to develop coping skills for winning and losing.

I Am Wonderfully Made!

GROWING

Day 1—God's works are amazing! And did you know you are one of His special works? He made you exactly like you are—wonderful! And He made you in His likeness. Isn't it grand to know that God made you like Him?

God made you to be able to do many things. He gave you eyes to see all the bright colors of the world, ears to hear birds singing and music playing, a nose for smelling sweet flowers or Grandma's freshly baked bread, a mouth for tasting that good bread Grandma bakes, and hands for feeling your new soft puppy. He gave you legs for running and walking. He gave you arms for reaching and hugging. And God gave you a mind, too! You use your mind to think and wonder about many different kinds of things.

What are some of the things you think and wonder about? Every day you use your mind, eyes, ears, nose, hands, and mouth to help you learn more and more about God's world.

Day 2—Did you know that God knows what you are thinking? God knows everything about you. He knows when you are happy and when you are sad. He knows when you are lonely. He also knows if you are angry! God made you, and you are His. He wants to take care of you, and He wants you to love Him.

There's no one exactly like you. Remember that. God made you just the way you are because that is how He wanted you to be—you. You are wonderfully made!

Now shout it out loud: "I am wonderfully made!"

Open the Bible, and read: I am wonderfully made (see Psalm 139:14); God gave us ears to hear and eyes to see (see

Proverbs 20:12); and love God (see Mark 12:30).

Say a prayer: Dear God, I am glad to be me! Thank You that I am wonderfully made. Help me to be like You in all that I do, think, and say. Amen.

On the Go

• Teach your child the familiar song, "Head and Shoulders." Then take up-close photos of your child's head, shoulders, knees, and toes. Mount each photo onto a small card. Laminate for durability. Mix up the cards and ask your preschooler to put his body parts in the correct order. This is also a fun activity to do if you have more than one child. Make a set of body parts cards for each child. Mix up the cards and ask each child sort his body parts. Lead him to put his head, shoulders, knees, and toes in order to make a complete body. Remind your child that he is wonderfully made.[1]

• Help your child make an I Am Special book. You will need scissors, yarn, 9-by-12-inch construction paper in different colors, ruler, hole punch, tempera paint, and markers. Fold a piece of construction paper in half. Cut 1/4 inch off the left side. Fold another piece of construction paper in half. Cut 1/2 inch off the left side. Fold another piece of construction paper in half. Cut 3/4 inch off the left side. Fold a fourth piece of construction paper in half. Cut 1 inch off the left side. Put the book together so it has indexlike pages. Punch holes on the left side of the booklet and tie together with yarn. Lead your child to draw and write about himself on each page. On the front of the booklet write, *I Am Special*.[2]

Growing and Changing

GROWING

When you were first born, someone had to hold you because you could not sit up by yourself. But you started to grow, and you learned to sit up. Before long you could crawl all over the place. Soon your legs were strong enough and you were ready to walk. Your mom and dad sometimes couldn't keep up with you because you could walk so fast!

When you were first born, you couldn't talk. You could cry though. Sometimes you could cry louder than any other baby around! As you grew, you learned to make funny little sounds and cute smiles too. Next thing you know, you were able to laugh out loud and have silly giggles with your friends. And you were talking (and talking and talking)!

When you were first born, your little hands were very tiny and so were your feet. But you had all ten fingers and ten toes. It wasn't long before your feet and hands grew. You were able to hold a drinking cup with your hands. Your feet had to have new shoes because they were growing so fast. Your feet and legs worked hard as you pedaled your new riding toy.

Every day you are growing and changing. Your body is growing on the outside and it's growing on the inside too!

Open the Bible, and read: God made us (see Psalm 100:3), and God made me (see Psalm 139:14).

Say a prayer: Thank You, God, that I am growing every day. Thank You for my body and help it to keep growing inside and outside just as You planned. Amen.

ON THE GO

•As a family, look at photos of your child. Show him pictures

of various stages of his life from birth to his age now. Talk about how your child has grown and how his body has changed since he was first born. Help your child make a sequence chart using the photos to show his stages of growth. At the top of the chart, write, *Look How I'm Growing!* Suggest your child glue the photos in order to show how he has grown. Underneath each photo, help him list the things he could do at each stage. Display the chart and each day talk to your child about how his body is growing on the outside as well as the inside.

• Teach your child to sing this song to the tune of "(Here We Go 'Round) the Mulberry Bush."

> *Growing and growing and changing too.*
> *Look at me. Look at you.*
> *Inside and out, that is the way*
> *We're growing and changing every day.*

Taking Care of My Body

GROWING

Day 1—Your body is growing and changing, and God wants you to take good care of your body. There are many ways you can take care of your body. You can get plenty of rest. Growing bodies need lots of sleep to help them grow properly. You can eat good healthy food that will help your body grow and stay well. You can exercise to keep your muscles and bones strong. You can brush your teeth and your hair. You can take a bath every day to keep your body clean. And you can wash your hands before you eat a meal or your favorite snack.

Once there was a boy named Daniel. Daniel's family was a rich Jewish family. But King Nebuchadnezzar and his army destroyed the city where Daniel and his family lived. The king took some of the Jews and made them into slaves. Daniel and some of his friends were in that group. They were prisoners, but the king needed a few of the boys to learn how to serve him. So the king sent the boys to a special school. The king ordered the boys to eat really fancy foods, but Daniel had learned as a young boy that he should not eat these foods. He had learned as a little boy that God's people were to eat only certain types of foods that were healthy. He begged the king's helper, "Please, sir, let me have only fresh vegetables and fruits to eat and water to drink. These foods are good for my body."

The king's helper worried that the king would be mad if Daniel didn't eat what the king had ordered. He worried that Daniel might become weak or even get sick. But he finally agreed to let Daniel and his friends eat only the fresh vegetables and fruits and drink water, but only for ten days.

Day 2—After the ten days, Daniel and his friends looked

better and healthier than anyone else. They showed the king's helper how strong they were as they exercised in front of him. Their eyes sparkled and they had bright smiles. They had more energy than any of the other boys. The king's helper couldn't believe it.

Daniel and his friends were allowed to keep eating the healthy foods they wanted. They grew to be strong, smart, and very wise. They took care of their bodies by eating good foods, exercising, and studying hard.

After three years, the king selected Daniel and his friends to be his special helpers. They were glad that they were no longer slaves, but could work for the king. They were glad too that they could take care of their bodies like God wanted them to do. God was happy that Daniel and his friends took good care of their bodies by eating good food, exercising, and getting plenty of rest.

Open the Bible, and read: God gives food to us (see Psalm 136:25).

For further reading, read Daniel 1:1–6.

Say a prayer: Dear God, thank You for my body. Help me to take care of my body by eating healthy foods that You give me. Help me to stay strong and happy. Amen.

On the Go
•Go grocery shopping with your child. Together talk about healthy foods and let your child help you pick out fresh vegetables and fruits to enjoy at home. Older preschoolers can begin to understand the basic food groups. Place a food pyramid chart in your kitchen or eating area. Ask your child to keep a list of what he eats during the day.
•Help your child draw an outline of his body. As he eats a food, save the wrapper, box top, or label. Suggest your child glue the wrappers and labels to his body outline. When the entire body outline is covered, talk about the kinds of foods

your child has eaten. Talk about how they help his body grow.

- Exercise together as a family. Take walks, go swimming, skate in the park, jump rope, ride bicycles, climb the jungle gym, or toss a ball.
- When traveling with your child, ask him to help you pack his favorite snacks. Make a Snack Pack Server. Pack a plastic serving dish with divided sections and a lid. Put dried fruit pieces, gelatin squares, celery sticks, crackers, or cookies in it. Place the lid on the plate until your child is ready to eat.[3]

Look at Me Learn!

GROWING

Day 1—You have been learning ever since you were a tiny little baby. God gave you a brain and a mind for learning. Do you know how you learn? You learn when you smell, taste, hear, see, and touch things. What do you like to smell? What do you like to taste? You also learn when you are doing things. What are some of the things you do every day? When you are playing, you are learning. Playing is fun, isn't it? And learning is fun too!

You learn by watching your mom and dad. You can learn when you play with your friends. You can learn by listening to your teachers too. All of the people around you help you learn. What are some of the things you have learned from the people in your family? What have you learned from your friends? What have you learned from your teachers?

You can learn by looking at books. When you look at pictures and hear stories from books, you can learn all about the world and the people and things in the world. What is your favorite book?

When you read your Bible, you can learn to be more like Jesus. How can you be like Jesus? When you help, show kindness, and love others, you are being like Jesus.

Day 2—Did you know you learn differently from everyone else? God made you to be just like you are. No two people learn exactly the same. You learn in ways that might be different from how your friends and family learn.

God wants you to use your mind and learn many new things. There are many things in the world that you can learn about. Explore and discover all the exciting things God has given you to enjoy.

Open the Bible, and read: God gives us things to enjoy (see 1 Timothy 6:17); God gave us ears to hear and eyes to see (see Proverbs 20:12); and I am wonderfully made (see Psalm 139:14).

Say a prayer: Dear God, I want to learn many new things. Help me to use my mind to learn more about You and all the good things You have given me to enjoy. Amen.

On the Go
•Provide opportunities for your child to use puzzles; sorting; sequencing and counting games; picture books; Bible story books; musical tapes; mobiles; sensory activities such as tasting new foods from other countries, hearing simple phrases in different languages, seeing pictures, etc.; a variety of art media; and a prop box for dress up and role play.
•Take your child to as many different places as possible. Visit the zoo, museums, and the library. Introduce your child to new people.

Parent Pointer
Become familiar with characteristics and learning styles of preschoolers.

Look What I Can Do!

GROWING

You have learned that you can do many things. You use your mind to learn many things. You can help others, work together, love others, be kind, pray, and give money to your church.

What are some other things you can do? Can you walk down the stairs by yourself? Can you tie your own shoes? Can you button your jacket? Can you write your name all by yourself? Do you know your ABC's? Can you climb a jungle gym? Wow! You can do many things. Look what all you can do!

God made you to do many things. Every day you are growing and learning to do more and more. Just think about what all you've learned to do since you were first born. Look at all you can do!

Open the Bible, and read: Give thanks to the Lord for He is good (see Psalm 107:1); God made us (see Psalm 100:3); love each other (see John 15:17); help one another (see Galatians 5:13); pray for one another (see James 5:16); be kind to one another (see Ephesians 4:32); and bring an offering (see 1 Chronicles 16:29).

Say a prayer: Dear God, thank You for making me able to do many things. I am glad that I can count, sing, tie my shoes, pray, ride my bicycle, and play with my friends. Help me as I keep learning to do more and more things. Amen.

ON THE GO

- Plan a Show-and-Tell night to celebrate all the things your child can do. Encourage your child to show or tell about what he can do. Videotape or take pictures as your child shows what he can do. You'll want to save these special memories.

120

I Can Make Choices

GROWING

You can make choices. Every day you are growing and learning more. You are learning to make choices. What are some choices you make?

When you get angry, or mad, what do you choose to do? Do you choose to use words instead of choosing to hit someone who might make you angry? It is good to choose words to talk things out. Hitting is not good, is it?

Do you choose to talk about how you feel, or do you go off by yourself and hide in your room? When you talk to someone about how you feel, you will usually feel better. You can also choose to talk to God about how you feel. God cares about how you feel.

Do you like to choose what clothes you will wear? Your mother may ask if you'd like to wear your red sweater or your yellow sweater. What will you choose?

Do you choose what to drink with your meals? Your dad may offer you juice or milk. What will you choose?

What activities do you like to choose to do at school or church? You can choose to sit quietly by yourself and read a book. You can choose to build a tower in the block center with your friends. You can choose to go into the homeliving area and pretend to be a doctor or a police officer. Or you might choose to paint a picture in the art area.

Sometimes your friends might want you to do something that you know is wrong. You can choose to do the wrong thing, or you can choose to do the right thing. God lets you make choices. And God is always there to help you make the right choices. God will help you know what to do. God will help you because He loves you. Isn't it good that you can make choices?

Open your Bible, and read: God cares for you (see 1 Peter 5:7), and I am wonderfully made (see Psalm 139:14).

Say a prayer: Dear God, thank You for letting me make choices. Help me to make the right choices every day. Amen.

On the Go

- Play the Choice Game with your family. Write each of the following choices on a separate strip of paper. Then place the paper strips into a box with an opening large enough for your child's hand to fit through. Each day ask your child to draw out one strip and to make a choice. Create and add new choice strips when the box is empty.
    1. What will you choose? To go outside and toss a ball to your parents or go on a nature walk?
    2. What will you choose? To watch your favorite television show or read your favorite book?
    3. What will you choose? To eat carrots and celery or apples and oranges?
    4. What will you choose? To listen to music or paint a picture?
    5. What will you choose? To make a card inviting a friend to church or call a friend and invite her to church?
- Help your child make choices while you are eating out, visiting the library, going to church, or playing with friends. Each day talk about all the choices you and your child make. Remind your child that God will help you both to make good choices.
- Play the Choice Game while riding in the car. Will we listen to the radio or to a cassette tape? Will we take this road or that one? Will we stop and eat hamburgers or pizza?

I Can Share

GROWING

God wants you to share with others. But sharing is sometimes not a very easy thing to do, is it? You want to keep your toys, books, games, puzzles, and all of your belongings safe. You want to have things just for yourself and no one else. God understands how you feel about your things. And it's OK to have some things that are yours and yours only. But God wants you to share what you can with others. What are some of the things you can share?

Can you share your toys with your friends when they come to your house to play? If you do not want them to play with certain toys, then you might put away those toys in a safe place until your friends leave.

Can you share some of your food with others? When you take canned goods or boxed food items to a food pantry, you are sharing with others. You might ask your mom or dad to buy some extra canned goods this week when they do the grocery shopping so you can take those to someone who needs food. Or maybe you can make a fruit basket to share with someone who is not feeling well.

You can share your clothes too. Did you know there are some children who do not have warm clothes to wear in the winter? You could take the clothes that you outgrow and give them to some of these children.

You might like to share some of your books you no longer read. You can give these to a homeless shelter or to a school that might not have many books for young children.

You do not have to share everything you have, but share what you can with others. When you share with others, you are being like Jesus.

Open the Bible, and read: God gives us things to enjoy (see

1 Timothy 6:17); be kind to one another (see Ephesians 4:32); help one another (see Galatians 5:13); and share what you have (see 2 Corinthians 8:4).

Say a prayer: Dear God, sometimes I don't like to share my things, but I want to be kind like You said I should be. Teach me to learn to share my things. Help me to share what I have with others. Amen.

ON THE GO

- Make a Share Box. Provide a medium-sized box or a laundry basket. Lead your child to place toys, books, games, or other items in the box so he can share them with his friends when they come to play. Remind your child that sharing what he has with others is important. When your child's friends come over, bring out the Share Box. Gradually add new items to the box when your child feels he can "let go." Place special toys that your child is not ready to share in a separate box or basket and keep these in a private place when friends visit.
- Work together to clean out your child's closet. Take clothing that your child can no longer wear or toys that your child no longer plays with to a homeless shelter or to someone who is in need. Take your child with you to deliver the items. Talk about the importance of sharing after you make the delivery.
- Clean out your pantry and ask your child to help you pack a bag of canned goods and boxed food items. Take your child with you to deliver these to a needy family.
- Invite a family in your neighborhood who has young children to come for dinner. As everyone is serving his plate, emphasize how you are sharing a meal.
- Bring out your child's favorite toys and talk about taking turns. Help your child to know that it's OK for him to finish playing with the toy before giving it to someone else.
- Talk about your child's thoughts. Tell him that his thoughts

are his very own. Point out that he does not have to share his thoughts or feelings unless he wants to. Remind your child that he can always share his feelings with God because God is always ready to listen.

PARENT POINTER

Remember that a child is usually not developmentally ready to learn to share until he is about four years old. Learning to share is a gradual process. Remember, do not scold a child for not wanting to share, but be patient and speak kindly as you guide him. Be sure to offer sincere praise when your child is finally able to share a toy or game.

I Can Be Honest

GROWING

Day 1—You can be honest. Being honest means knowing what is real and what is not real. Sometimes it can be hard to know what is real and what is not real, can't it? But you must try to understand what is real and what isn't because God wants you to be honest at all times.

Sometimes you can have lots of fun being silly and pretending. When you dress up as a nurse, police officer, or firefighter, are you really one? No. Of course you're not. You are just pretending to be one, right? You are still a little child. But one day you will grow up, and you might become a nurse or police officer. It's OK to pretend when you are playing, but just because you pretend to be a nurse or a police officer doesn't mean that you are.

Do you like telling made-up stories sometimes? You might have told someone that your mother was a queen who lived in a castle. Or you could have told a friend that when you went fishing with your dad, you caught a gigantic whale. You know you really didn't catch a big whale or that your mother is not really a queen, but it's fun making up stories and pretending.

Remember, though, just because you tell something (and even if you tell it over and over again), that doesn't mean that it is true or that it will come true. You might wish it could come true, but it probably will not.

Day 2—God gave you something called an imagination. You pretend with your imagination. You can wish for things. You can think about faraway places you've never seen. And you can let your imagination go on and on and on. Using your imagination can be fun, but using your imagination is not always what is real.

Remember the commandment you learned about telling the truth? God wants you to tell the truth and be honest when you are not playing or pretending. If you are confused about what is real and what is not real, talk to your mom and dad. They can help you to know the difference as you grow and change and learn.

Open the Bible, and read: Always tell the truth (see Exodus 20:12).

Say a prayer: Dear God, help me to know the difference between what is real and what is not real. I always want to tell the truth and be honest. Amen.

ON THE GO
•Join your child in make-believe play while he's playing with his toys. Talk to him about pretending after you finish playing. Watch an age-appropriate TV program or video with your child. Talk about the difference between make-believe and what is really true.
•Encourage your child to pretend he is an elephant, a clown, a rocket, a king, or a queen. When pretend time is over, remind him that he really is not the thing he pretended to be.
•Confront your child when you overhear him telling someone something that is not true. Tell him that it's OK to pretend if the other person knows he's pretending, but it's not OK to pretend if someone else believes him.
•Model honesty for your child. Compliment your child's honesty.

The Giving Me

GROWING

Day 1—Learning to give is an important part of growing up. The Bible tells us that God loves a cheerful giver (see 2 Corinthians 9:7). That means that God wants you to give to others and be happy about doing it. What are some things you can give to others?

You can give your money to your church. The money you give to your church helps the people who work in your church. Some of the money you give goes to help missionaries. A missionary is a person who goes to many different places to tell others about Jesus. Some of the money you give helps people who do not have as much as you have. The Bible also tells us to bring an offering to church (see Malachi 3:10). When you go to church, you can take some of your money and put it in the offering plate. God is happy when you give money to help your church.

You can give your time too. When you give your time, you do things for other people. It takes time to travel to visit a shut-in at the nursing home, but the person in the nursing home is so happy that you took the time to come see him. You can give your time when you help do chores around the house or make a card and send it to a sick friend. You can take time to bake cookies for your new neighbor.

You can give your love. When you smile and give someone a hug, you give him love. You can take time to tell others that you love them, too. And you can tell them that Jesus loves them. Jesus said, "I love you" (see John 15:9).

Day 2—You can give things to help people. You can give food to people who do not have enough to eat. You can give clothes to people who do not have enough to wear. You can give a pencil to someone in your class who may not have

one. You can draw a picture and give it to your mom or dad. You can give someone a birthday or Christmas present too.

You can give thanks to God. God has given you so much, and it is good to give Him thanks for all He has done. When you pray, you can give thanks to God. When you sing, you can give thanks to God. When you play with your friends, you can give thanks to God.

Have you ever received a gift? How did it make you feel? When you give to others, they feel like you do when you receive a gift. Happy! The more you learn to give, the more you are able to help others. You can give your money. You can give your time. You can give your love. You can give things. You can give thanks to God. Why, just look at you! You can give and give and give. That makes God very happy.

Open the Bible, and read: God loves a cheerful giver (see 2 Corinthians 9:7); bring an offering to church (see Malachi 3:10); it is a good thing to give thanks to God (see Psalm 92:1); and Jesus said, "I love you" (see John 15:9).

Say a prayer: Thank You, God, for all You give me to enjoy. Teach me that it is better to give than to receive. Amen.

ON THE GO
- Read *The Giving Tree* by Shel Silverstein together as a family. Talk about the importance of giving and different ways your family can give to help others.
- Help your child make a coin bank from a small box. Lead him to use a marker to decorate the box. Cut a slit in the top of the box so a coin can fit through it. Each week give your child some money, and encourage him to save part of it. He can give it to a church, a homeless shelter, or a local charity.
- Help your child make fabric cards. Provide small scraps of fabric, yarn, ribbon, lace, and markers. Give your child a

piece of construction paper and lead him to fold it in half to make a card. Suggest he glue the fabric scraps and other items to the front of the card. Inside, help your child write a message to someone to whom he'll send the card. When he has finished with the card, talk about how he felt making something special to give to someone he loves.[4]

•When you buy gifts for someone's birthday, anniversary, or Christmas, take your child shopping with you and let him help pick out a gift that he can give. Help him wrap the gift and ask your child to make a special presentation when he gives the gift to the person.

•Take a walk with your child. Tell him that today you will be giving smiles away. Encourage your child to smile at every person he sees.

Making Friends

GROWING

Day 1—It's easy to make friends. You can invite someone to come and play with you at your house or you can go to the playground and play. Maybe you'd like to work a puzzle at school with one of your friends. The two of you can put the puzzle pieces together and then enjoy a snack. You can laugh and talk about other things you like to do. You can have both girls and boys as your friends. Sometimes you have friends for a very short time and sometimes you will have friends for a very long time.

The Bible tells us about two good friends. Their names were David and Jonathan. David and Jonathan knew from the very first time they met that they would be friends forever. They would be best friends. Jonathan loved David, and David loved Jonathan. When the boys grew up and became strong men, Jonathan saved David's life by protecting him and hiding him from King Saul who wanted to kill David.

You see, friends love each other. They help each other and work together. They are kind to each other.

Day 2—Jesus wants you to be one of His friends. The Bible tells you that Jesus said, "You are my friends" (see John 15:14). The Bible also tells you that a friend loves at all times (see Proverbs 17:17). How can you be friends with Jesus? How do you know that Jesus is your friend?

God is happy when you make friends. Keep your old friends. Make new friends. Remember Jesus is your friend. He loves you at all times.

Open the Bible, and read: A friend loves at all times (see Proverbs 17:17); Jesus said, "You are my friends" (see John 15:14); and Jesus had friends (see Luke 2:52).

For further reading, read 1 Samuel 18:1–4; 19:1–7.

Say a prayer: Dear God, thank You, for giving me friends. Help me to be a good friend to others as I show them love and help them. Thank You for sending Jesus to be my friend and to love me at all times. Amen.

ON THE GO
• Invite young children to come and play with your child. Have a special day each week when a friend or friends can come to play at your house.
• As a family, get to know your child's friends and their families. Invite families for dinner, coffee, or to come to church with you.
• Model how you can make friends. Let your child see you having fun with, sharing, and being kind to your friends.
• Lead your child to string colorful beads onto a piece of yarn, ribbon, or cord to make a friendship bracelet that he can give to a friend. As he makes the bracelet, teach him this song sung to the tune of "I'm a Little Teapot."
> *I can be a friend like Jesus said to be.*
> *Showing love to others and sharing happily.*
> *Friends help one another and are so kind.*
> *Working together, I love these friends of mine!*

*Grand*friends

GROWING

Your mom and dad have parents too. They are your grand-parents and they love you very much. You may live near your grandparents or you might live very far from them. If you live close to them, you may see them often and get to do special things with them. If you live far away from them, you may still get to do special things with them, but just not as often.

You may have friends who are like your grandparents especially if your real grandparents live far away from you. These are your "grandfriends." No, they can't ever take the place of the special feelings you have for your grandparents, but they can still care for you and love you too.

Grandfriends might teach your class at church or help in your preschool or kindergarten. A grandfriend might be a neighbor you help or visit. You might take walks with your grandfriend or you might like to play games, sing songs, or help carry groceries for her.

Once there was a young boy named Samuel. He had a grandfriend named Eli. Eli was a priest at the tabernacle. (A priest is like a preacher. A tabernacle is like a church.) Eli and Samuel spent a lot of time with each other. They would talk and talk. Eli loved Samuel, and Samuel loved Eli too. Samuel worked at the tabernacle. He opened the doors, cleaned the furniture, and swept the floor. Samuel loved working in the tabernacle because Eli would teach him many things about God. Samuel was learning to become a priest like Eli.

Samuel grew up to love God very much. He told the people what God wanted them to do and how much God loved them. God sends us friends of all ages. Samuel was glad to have Eli as his grandfriend. Your grandfriends can be some of the best friends you'll ever have. Thank God for them now.

Open the Bible, and read: A friend loves at all times (see Proverbs 17:17).
For further reading, read 1 Samuel 3. (Read only brief sections at one sitting with your child.)

Say a prayer: Dear God, thank You for all of my friends. I thank You especially for my grandfriends and how they help me. Show me ways I can help them too. Amen.

ON THE GO
•Help your child make friends with senior adults including his grandparents. Invite a senior adult in your neighborhood or from your church to come to your home for dinner. If possible, and if you know the person well, ask the grandfriend to baby-sit when you must be away from your child.
•Make friendship cookies to take to your child's grandfriend. You'll need 1/3 cup honey; 1 tablespoon oil; 1/2 teaspoon salt; 1 tablespoon orange rind, grated; 2 eggs; and 1 1/2 cups oatmeal. Mix the first three ingredients. Add the next three to the mixture. Drop by spoonfuls on oiled cookie sheet. Bake at 400°F for 8 minutes. Take the cookies to your grandfriend to say thank you for being a terrific grandfriend.[5]

When I Get Mad

GROWING

Have you ever been mad at someone? What did you do? Did you want to yell at him? Or throw something? Did you hold up your fist? Did you hit that person? Or maybe you were so angry that you just decided to bite them, and bite them hard!

Everyone gets mad at times. It is important, though, that you know what to do when you get mad. You do not have to yell, hit, or bite. You can think about what to do before you do something that will hurt another person.

You can use words. Talk things out. Tell that person that you didn't like how he made you feel. When you use kind words, you will not hurt someone. When you use kind words, you do not have to raise your voice either. You can speak to a person in your normal voice. If someone is doing something to you that you do not like, it's OK to shout, "Stop that!"

Sometimes at first you might be too angry to talk it out. You don't feel like talking to anyone. When you'd rather not talk, you can draw a picture showing how you feel. You can call this picture your angry picture. You can build a tower of blocks and knock them down. You can pound some clay to make an angry sculpture. None of these will hurt others or destroy anything.

You should never hurt someone just because you are angry. And you should not tear up something or break something because you are mad either. That doesn't help at all.

You can pray. God will help you not to feel so angry. God understands and He knows all about you. He knows exactly how you feel.

Open your Bible, and read: Be kind to one another (see Ephesians 4:32).

Say a prayer: Dear God, help me when I'm so mad that I don't know what to do. Help me not to hurt anyone or to tear up anything. Please give me the right words to say and to know the right things to do when I'm feeling angry. Amen.

ON THE GO
- Make up simple songs about how your child is feeling when he is angry.
- Make puppets from paper bags or socks, or use an old glove to make finger puppets. Lead your child to decorate the puppets and then ask him to use the puppets to tell about what happened and why he is so angry. Let him demonstrate what happened to make him so mad as he uses one of the puppets. Then talk to him about what words he could use to solve the problem. Ask him to use the puppets to show what he would do.

PARENT POINTER
Model self-control as you choose words and actions when you are frustrated or angry. Teach your child to use words when he gets angry. Make sure he understands that it is not acceptable to destroy things or hurt someone. If your child has trouble learning to handle his anger, seek professional help.[6]

I Have Feelings Too

GROWING

Everybody has feelings. How you feel about things might be very different from how your friends or family members feel. Your feelings are your very own. How do you let someone know how you are feeling?

Have you ever felt angry? You have learned that it's OK to get angry. But it's not OK to hurt someone or destroy things, is it?

Have you ever felt sad? You might cry when you are sad, or you might feel all alone. You can use puppets to "talk" to each other about why you are sad too.

Have you ever felt scared? Maybe you had a bad dream or your mom turned off the lights and it was very dark in your room. You might have seen something on television that scared you.

Have you ever done something that you thought was bad? Were you worried that someone would find out about what you did? What did you think would happen?

Do you ever feel happy? When you're happy, do you laugh out loud? Do you like to skip and sing songs when you're happy? Do you like to act silly when you're happy?

There are all kinds of feelings—good ones and sometimes not so good ones too. With every kind of feeling you have, you can talk to your parents, your teachers, or your friends. They love you and they can help you feel better. They can help you deal with your feelings. Do you know who else can help you with your feelings? God can! God gave you feelings. He knows that everything that happens to you will affect how you feel in some way. You can tell God about your feelings. God will listen. God listens to you because He cares for you.

Open the Bible, and read: God cares for you (1 Peter 5:7); and when I am afraid, I will trust in God (see Psalm 56:3).

Say a prayer: Dear God, thank You for giving me feelings. Help me to know what to do when I feel sad, scared, angry, or when I've done something I shouldn't do. Thank You for happy feelings . Thank You for Jesus too. Jesus makes me feel happy. Amen.

ON THE GO

•Play a game of How Do You Feel? Provide a paper plate and from construction paper cut out several facial features representing different feelings. Lay the features aside. Give your child the plate, and ask him to choose and put on the plate the facial features that show how he would feel if:

  he were going to a new school;
  he had broken his mother's favorite vase;
  he were alone in a dark room;
  he had just received a present from a friend;
  he fell and scraped his knee.

•A fun book to share together as a family is *Today I Feel Silly and Other Moods That Make My Day* by Jamie Lee Curtis.

PARENT POINTER

Reassure your child that you have feelings too. Talk about what makes you sad, scared, angry, and happy. Pray about the things that make you afraid and commit them to God.

Where's My Mommy?

GROWING

Sometimes your mom or dad might have to leave you for a short while. They might have to go to work while you go to preschool or kindergarten. They might have to go to a doctor's office while you stay with a friend. They might have to go with other grown-ups to a party while you stay with a sitter. Or they might go to their own Sunday School class or worship service at church while you stay with your friends in another room where you can learn about Jesus.

How do you feel about your parents leaving you? Do you wonder why you cannot be with your mom or dad? Do you worry that they are not coming back to get you? Do you really miss them a lot? Maybe, just maybe, you get angry at them for leaving you with someone. Do you feel like crying when your parents leave you?

Well, these feelings are OK. But you must remember you are growing and you are becoming a big boy or a big girl. Your mom and dad love you very much, and they will only leave you when they have to. They will always come back to get you because you are very important to them.

God loves you, and God cares about you too. The next time your mom or dad must leave you, you can trust God to take care of them and you. You can trust God that they will come back. Your mom and dad love you. God loves you too!

Open your Bible, and read: God cares for me (see 1 Peter 5:7); God loves you (see Psalm 107:1); when I am afraid, I will trust in God (see Psalm 56:3); and love your father and mother (see Exodus 20:12).

Say a prayer: Dear God, sometimes I don't like it when my mommy or daddy must leave me. I feel scared and I worry

they might forget me. Help me to remember that they love me and they will come back for me. Thank You, God, for loving me too. Amen.

On the Go

- Encourage your child to role-play the following situations as he pretends he is a grown-up who must leave his child:
    1. Mom is going to work. The young child is left at a childcare center.
    2. The young child is starting his first day at preschool or kindergarten. Mom and Dad must leave for a while.
    3. Mom and Dad are going to a party for the night. The young child will stay with his grandparents until Mom and Dad come back.
    4. Dad is going on a business trip for two weeks.
- Cut a circle from poster board. Look for pictures in magazines that show parts of your child's day such as going to school, playing with friends, and taking a nap. Include a picture that shows Mom and Dad picking up a child. Glue these pictures around the circle. Use a brad to attach an arrow to the center of the circle. Encourage your child to move the arrow from one thing to the next on the circle while he is waiting for his mom or dad to come back.[7]

Parent Pointer

When you leave your child for any length of time, tell him where you are going and how long you'll be gone. Reassure him that you are coming back. Help your child understand that he will be safe and have fun with whomever you are leaving him. (Never leave your child with a stranger. Remember it takes time for a young child to make a connection with another adult.) Avoid long good-byes and always be on time to pick up your child. If you are leaving your child for the first time, be sure it's for a very short while. Gradually lengthen times of separation.

Cooperation Is for Me!

GROWING

You have already learned that working together with your friends and family is important. Did you know that there is another big word for working together? It is *cooperation.* When you work together, or *cooperate,* you learn to share and take turns. You begin to think about ways to solve problems. When you cooperate, you know you are growing and changing.

Babies can't really work together, can they? No, they are much too young. Even a two-year-old is still too young. But you can begin to think about others. Soon you and your friends are thinking of ways you can work together to get things done.

You might work together with just one other person. At other times you might work with several friends. Together you can build a church building with the blocks. You might help each other and take turns turning the crank on an ice-cream freezer. You might put a puzzle together or work together to make cookies. You might work together to pick up apples or leaves that have fallen in your yard. Working together can be fun.

How will you cooperate with your friends? Your family? Your teachers?

Open the Bible, and read: We work together (see 1 Corinthians 3:9); help one another (see Galatians 5:13); and we are helpers (see 2 Corinthians 1:24).

Say a prayer: Dear God, I want to cooperate! When I cooperate with others, I know it makes You happy. Please help me to learn to work together with my friends, family, and teachers. Amen.

ON THE GO

• Have a family ball game to help young children learn the importance of cooperation and team spirit. Play a game called Newcomb. (It's similar to volleyball, except it's more appropriate for young children.) You will need a ball, a portable volleyball net that can be placed low to the ground, and colored chalk or tape. Go outside. As a family, work together to mark off an area about a third the size of a volleyball court. Place the low net in, or just draw a line across, the center. Outline the court so everyone will know the boundaries. Divide your family into two teams. Each team should be on one side of the net or line.

Decide what team will throw the ball over the net first. Anyone on the other side of the net may catch the ball, but it must be caught before it touches the ground. (Or it can be caught with only one bounce.) That person then in turn tosses the ball back over the net. The game continues until someone misses or the ball goes out of bounds. A team earns a point when the opposing team drops the ball or causes it to go out of bounds. Play until a team reaches 5 points. If interest persists, play another game, moving the winning points to 10. (In Newcomb, the game is over when a team reaches 21 points.)

Team members should encourage one another and help each other throughout the game. Have fun working together![8]

PARENT POINTER

Plan activities and provide toys that foster cooperation. Talk to your child about the importance of working together and helping others. Model cooperation as you help others.[9]

Learning to Get Along

GROWING

When you work together and cooperate, you are learning to get along with others. But sometimes you might have trouble learning to work together and get along. Has that ever happened to you? What if you and one of your friends want the same toy when you are playing? Or what if you both want the same ball or book? What can you do?

Jesus sometimes had problems with His friends too. Many times they did not understand what Jesus was doing. They would even get angry with Jesus sometimes. But Jesus wanted to help them understand. So He would think of ways to solve the problems.

Jesus thought of ways He could help His friends understand. He often told them stories to help them understand. Through His actions, Jesus always showed them how they should behave and what they should do even when it wasn't easy.

You can be like Jesus and be a problem solver too. Can you and your friend work it out when you are having a problem? Talk with each other about the problem. If a friend has done something that you do not like, tell him what it is. Think of at least one way to solve the problem. Think about what Jesus would do. If you are still having trouble, ask your mom or dad to help. If you are with other friends at church or in school, your teacher can help you. Ask your class to help you and your friend decide which solution to the problem will work best. Then together help each other solve the problem. Celebrate that you can solve problems and be like Jesus.

Open the Bible, and read: We work together (see 1 Corinthians 3:9); be kind to one another (see Ephesians 4:32); Jesus said

to love one another (see John 15:17); and Jesus went about doing good (see Acts 10:38).

Say a prayer: Dear God, I am glad that I can solve problems and be like Jesus. Before I try to solve a problem, help me to think about what Jesus would do. Amen.

ON THE GO

•Help your child to solve his problems as he experiences difficulty with others. As problems arise, talk about them with your child. Be available to help your child, but lead him to solve the problem himself. Ask: What's the problem? What can you do? What do you think Jesus would do? Be supportive, but try to avoid offering all the "right" answers as you help your child think. Lead your child to predict what he thinks will happen in a variety of situations. Establish a place in your home where your child can take his conflicts "to the table" and the family can offer collective conflict resolution.[10]

Learning to Say I'm Sorry

GROWING

Have you ever hurt someone's feelings or caused someone to be angry with you? Were you sorry later for how you treated that person? How do you feel when you are truly sorry for something? It's not easy to admit that you did something wrong, is it? But you can learn to say you are sorry. That will help you feel better about what you did. It will also help the person you hurt. What kind of things can you do to show you are sorry?

In the Bible, Jesus told a story about a man who had two sons. The youngest son did not want to obey his father. He just wanted his father's money. His father knew he was unhappy, so the father decided to give this son half of his money, hoping that would make him happier. But it didn't. The son took the money and ran away from home. Soon all of the money the son had taken with him was gone. He spent it on fancy parties and lots of expensive food. He never wrote a letter to his father or older brother to let them know he was OK. They thought he might be dead.

One day the youngest son decided he wanted to go back home. He was worried, though, that his father would be angry with him. But on his way back home, the son was so surprised. When his father saw him coming, he started to run toward his son. He had his arms wide open. The father hugged his son. He was so glad to see him. The son was sorry for what he had done. The father was happy to forgive him.

Open the Bible, and read: Love one another (see John 15:17); be kind to one another (see Ephesians 4:32); if we tell God what we have done wrong, He will forgive us (see 1 John 1:9); and be quick to forgive others (see Matthew 6:14).

For further reading, read Luke 15:11–24.

Say a prayer: Dear God, I want to be kind and love others. If I hurt my friends and family, please help me to tell them that I am sorry. Help me to learn to forgive those who hurt me too. Thank You, God, for forgiving me when I do wrong. Amen.

ON THE GO
- As a family, be quick to say I'm sorry to each other. Talk about the mistake together and next time try not to make the same mistake again. After your child has said he is sorry, encourage him to hug the person he has hurt. Suggest he draw the person a picture to show what he likes about her.
- As a family, talk about ways God forgives you when you do wrong. Praise God for loving you always, even when you make mistakes.

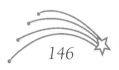

Have Patience! Don't Be in Such a Hurry!

GROWING

It's hard to wait for things to happen, especially if you are excited. Have you ever planned a trip and you were so excited that you couldn't wait to go? Learning to wait for things is part of growing up. When you wait calmly and do not complain, you are showing *patience*. God wants you to have patience.

You can show patience when you do not rush and take your time to do things the right way. You can take your time when painting a picture at school. You can take your time learning to tie your shoes or zip up your jacket. It takes time to learn to do things well.

You can show patience when things aren't going just like you want them to. You might want to play with a toy while someone else is playing with it. You can show patience while you wait for your turn.

You can show patience when you are sick. When you are sick, you must rest and take care of yourself so you can feel well again. You must slow down and wait until your body is well again.

A man in the Bible named Job was patient. He loved God very much. Job knew that whatever happened to him, God would take care of him and help him. Job was patient to wait on God. Job was very sick for a long time, but he was patient to wait on God to help him. No matter what happens or what you want to happen, have patience.

Open the Bible, and read: Have patience (see Galatians 5:22).

147

Say a prayer: Dear God, help me as I learn to wait for all the good things You have for me. Teach me to be patient even when it's not easy. Amen.

ON THE GO

- Go on a short fishing trip with your family. Talk about how it sometimes takes a long time to catch a fish. As you wait for the catch, talk about patience. When you catch a fish, celebrate your accomplishments. (Be sure to throw the fish back in the lake or pond.)
- At the movies, stand in line to buy tickets as a family. Explain to your child why you are waiting. Talk about the importance of patience as you wait in line.
- Talk with your child about other times he has had to wait such as at the doctor's office, at the bus or subway stop, for his parents to come pick him up, or for his favorite aunt to arrive for a visit.
- Make your child's favorite cookies together. Set the timer and allow the cookies to bake. Listen to the ticking on the timer. As the cookies bake, talk about waiting. After the cookies are ready and have cooled, thank God for good food to eat. Enjoy a cookie together. As you wait for the cookies to get ready, sing this song to the tune of "Row, Row, Row Your Boat."

> *Wait, wait, wait I can*
> *While the cookies bake.*
> *Wait, wait, wait again.*
> *Patience it will take.*

Those Things I Do Over and Over Again—Habits!

GROWING

Everyone has habits. A habit is something that you do over and over again without really thinking about what you are doing. Because you are different from your friends, your habits are probably different too. Take time to stop a few minutes and think about the things you do over and over again. What are some of your habits? How do your habits help you? How do your habits hurt you?

Brushing your teeth, taking a bath every day, eating your meals, going to school, playing with your toys and your friends, and saying your prayers are good habits that help.

Sometimes you might do things over and over again because you are worried about something. Do you bite your fingernails? Do you suck your thumb? Do you pull or twist your hair? Do you chew on your long-sleeved shirts? When you do these things, your mom and dad may tell you to stop. You may try to stop, but it isn't easy, is it? When your parents tell you to stop, does it make you feel bad? Well, that is not what they want to do. They just care about you very much and want to help you.

When something is bothering you, your parents can help you. Talk to them and tell them how you feel. In time, you will feel better and probably be able to stop those habits that might hurt you.

God cares about you too. He knows when something is bothering you. You can tell God all about your feelings, worries, and fears. And God listens when you talk to Him.

Open the Bible, and read: God cares for you (see 1 Peter 5:7), and God hears me when I pray (see 1 John 5:14).

Say a prayer: Dear God, thank You that I am learning many good habits that I will keep with me always. When I am worried, help me to remember that my parents care about me and can help me. Thank You for caring about me too. I know You will always be there to help me. Amen.

ON THE GO

- Encourage the good habits that your child has. Call them to his attention; tell him why these habits are good and that you are proud of him.
- To help relieve stress that causes certain harmful habits, lead your child to listen to quiet music, look at a favorite picture book, or paint a picture.
- Help soothe your child when he is anxious or worried. Suggest your child take a bubble bath as he plays with his favorite bath toys. Petting a kitten or puppy can also be helpful. Hold your child closely as you rock him, and sing this song to the tune of "Twinkle, Twinkle, Little Star."

> *Do you know that I love you?*
> *I love you no matter what you do.*
> *Mommy and Daddy, they love you so.*
> *God loves you too, He wants you to know.*
> *He will calm you when you are scared.*
> *God always loves you. God always cares.*

PARENT POINTER

Recognize what stresses or pressures are causing your child to bite his nails or pull his hair. Avoid criticizing and nagging, as this will only worsen the problem. Calmly talk to your child about what might be bothering him.

Winning and Losing

GROWING

Day 1—Do you like to win when you play games? Of course you do! Everyone likes to win. But what happens when you don't win and you lose a game? What then? How does that make you feel? It's hard when you lose a game. Winning is much more fun, but sometimes you will lose and it won't be much fun.

There will be times that you win and times that you lose. When you win, you can be happy and celebrate. When you lose, you can be happy for the other person who won. That can be hard, but you can do it. When you lose, you can talk about how it makes you feel. Your mom and dad can tell you about times they may have lost at a game too. It might be kind of hard talking about how you feel; so if you want, you can wait until you are feeling better and talk then. You can tell God how you are feeling. God knows how you feel when you win. He knows how you feel when you lose too. He loves you and cares about your feelings.

Day 2—Matthew liked taking karate lessons. He wanted more than anything to win the karate competitions. At one competition, though, Matthew was doing some of the karate movements when he fell on the ground. His leg was hurt; and he felt like crying because he knew when he fell, he had lost. Matthew was disappointed, but he knew he had done his very best. And you know what? Matthew did not give up trying. He kept going to karate and practicing and learning more and more. Sometimes he would win at competitions. Other times he would lose. When he became a teenager, Matthew earned his black belt in karate. That is the highest rank one can receive in karate.

Winning and losing is part of growing up. Sometimes

you will win at things you do and other times you will lose. But the important thing is that you do your very best whether you are playing a game with a friend, helping your family with chores, running in a race at school, or competing in a karate competition. Always do your best.

Open the Bible, and read: Never give up (see Galatians 6:9).

Say a prayer: Dear God, help me to be strong and never give up. Help me to be happy when I win and to keep trying when I lose. Help me to do my best always. Amen.

ON THE GO
- Celebrate wins and losses with your family. Help your child understand that even though he may have lost at a game, the important thing is that he put forth his best effort. Build your child's self-esteem when he loses at something by pointing out other times he has won. Encourage your child by taking him out and tossing or kicking a ball to him.
- Have family relay races in your backyard. Remind your child that sometimes he will win and other times he will lose. Talk about the importance of good sportsmanship and giving your best when you play a game.

Part V

Growing in Today's World

PARENT POINTERS
- Be prepared to answer your child's questions about divorce.
- Offer care and comfort to your child when he is sick and help him cope with his illness.
- Provide support and love to your child when his pet dies.
- Help your child cope with the death of a family member or friend. Be honest when answering a child's questions about death.
- Help your child understand what happens when your family must move.
- Teach your child that manners matter. Guide him to have good manners.
- Encourage your child to celebrate differences among all God's people.
- Teach your child to understand and accept disabilities.
- Limit your child's time with TV, computers, and videos. Know what programs your child watches and what games he plays.
- Lead your child to understand that he has responsibilities.
- Talk to your child when he hears about people who do bad things. Offer support, comfort, and coping skills if someone has hurt your child.
- Help your child know how he can take care of the earth.
- Teach your child the importance of work. Help your child know more about your workplace.
- Lead your child to be aware that sometimes people lose their jobs. Guide your child to think of ways to help.
- Teach your child acceptable words he can use. Help him choose good words to say.
- Consider giving your young child an allowance to help him

learn more about money. Begin teaching him money management at an early age. Stress the importance of giving.
- Recognize when your child is being bullied or teased. Help him deal with self-esteem issues that may arise from the teasing and bullying.
- Encourage your child to try new things and to keep trying as he learns how to do them.
- Help your child cope in frightening times. If he has heard the word *terrorism*, talk to him about what it means. Help him to understand *war* when he asks about it.

Why Did Mom and Dad Get a Divorce?

GROWING

Day 1—You may have heard the word *divorce*. Divorce means that two people who are married decide they no longer want to be married to each other. They do not want to live together anymore as a husband and a wife.

Perhaps you know a friend whose parents are divorced or maybe your own parents are divorced. Did you know that some boys and girls think that they caused their parents to divorce? But do you know what? Children do not cause their parents to divorce. When a mom and dad divorce, they may no longer love each other. There can be many reasons for this happening, but they will never stop loving their children. Parents love their children forever.

Day 2—Some children worry that the parent who moved away after a divorce will not come back and visit. They feel lonely and sad and miss that parent very much. Most parents who have to move away come back for regular visits. They are so happy to have time with their children. Some children worry that the parent they are living with may leave them too. That is not going to happen. Parents know that their children need to live with at least one parent. When parents get a divorce, they decide where the children will live. Both parents want to take good care of the children.

God can help families who have been through a divorce. He can help the parents know the right things to do for their children. God cares about all kinds of families even when the mom and dad no longer live together. God cares for the children in these families too. Families who divorce should

spend time praying and asking God to help them do the right things.

Divorce is not easy for families. When divorce happens, everyone in the family has all kinds of feelings. They might be sad, angry, or confused, but God is always there to help. God loves everyone. Nothing will ever change that. God will love you and your mom and dad always.

Open the Bible, and read: God cares for you (see 1 Peter 5:7), and God loves us always (see Psalm 107:1).

For further reading, read Matthew 19:3–11 and Mark 10:2–9.

Say a prayer: Dear God, I thank You for my family. I pray for families whose moms and dads are divorced. Help them to know the right thing to do for each other and for their children. Thank You, God, for caring about my family and me. Thank You for loving us too. Amen.

On the Go

- If you experience divorce, always be honest with your child without creating fear or blaming the other parent.
- Help your child deal with his feelings of guilt. Make sure he knows the divorce is not his fault.
- Establish routine visits for the parent who must move out or away from the child.
- Provide lots of reassurance, security, and love.
- Allow your child to visit both sets of grandparents if at all possible.
- Be sensitive to a child who may seem unaffected by the divorce. Often regression and withdrawal are common when divorce affects a young child.
- If you are a parent who must move away from your child, be sure to call and send cards, a video, or email often. Record a message on a cassette tape and send this to your child too.

157

- Help your child make a card or booklet for the parent who had to move away. Or suggest he draw a picture.
- Always speak positively about the other parent.
- Keep in touch with your child and make sure to attend special events in his life. If you can't be there, call him.
- Make a special Parent and Child Cookbook with fun recipes a dad or a mom can use with their child when he comes for visits.[1]

I Don't Feel Well!

GROWING

Day 1—Have you ever had a stomachache? How about a bad cold or sore throat? Being sick is no fun, is it? When you are sick, you may not feel like playing with your friends. You may not want to eat like you usually do. You may want to stay in the bed or snuggle closely with your favorite teddy bear. Sometimes you might feel fussy, cranky, or even sad; and that's OK too. God knows when you are sick. He cares for you.

Sometimes when you are sick, you might go to the hospital. Have you ever been to the hospital? Going to the hospital might be scary, but it doesn't have to be. Remember God sends people to help take care of you and make you feel better while you are there. Doctors and nurses help. Your mother and father and other family members can help.

Sometimes you might have a friend who helps when you are sick. They all want to help you feel better because they love you and care about you. They are doing what the Bible says. They are helping each other. God wants to help you feel better too.

Day 2—Once Jesus helped a group of men who had a skin disease called leprosy. It caused these men to have sores all over their bodies. People who had leprosy covered their heads and bodies so no one would see their ugly sores. When the men saw Jesus, they begged Him to please heal their skin. Jesus saw them and said, "Go and show yourselves to the people in the church." The men did what Jesus said, and as they were walking toward the church, they looked at their skin. There were no more sores! Jesus made them well. They jumped for joy and went into the church shouting and thanking Jesus for making them well.

Jesus made these men well, and He also made many

other people well too. He still does this today. But sometimes people do not get well. They can be sick for a very long time. Still God has a plan for every person's life. And God has a plan for the sick person too.

Open the Bible, and read: We are helpers (see 2 Corinthians 1:24); help one another (see Galatians 5:13); and Jesus made sick people well (see Luke 7:21).
For further reading, read Luke 17:11–16.

Say a prayer: God, thank You for caring when I am sick. Please help people who are sick to feel better. Help doctors and nurses know the best way to help sick people who are in the hospital. Amen.

ON THE GO
- If your child is sick, expect him to feel cranky and fussy. Be patient and try to spend time with him. If you work outside the home, if at all possible, try to stay home with your child during his illness.
- If your child goes to the hospital, read *Going to the Hospital* by Fred Rogers. Help your child role-play feelings about going to the hospital. Look through a child's doctor's or nurse's kit. Talk about the instruments and how a doctor or nurse might use them.
- Place a basket of activity books next to your child's bed. Provide crayons, markers, or pencils. Also provide picture books and his favorite cassette tapes and CDs.
- Pray with your child for people you know who are sick. Make get-well cards, pick a bouquet of flowers to give them, or bake cookies to take to them.
- Suggest your child phone a sick friend or help him find an electronic card to send to a friend.
- If you know of a child who suffers with a chronic illness, suggest that the family find a support group for help.

PARENT POINTERS

Keep a child home when he has:

1. any physical or emotional condition that would prevent him from participating comfortably in class.
2. a fever of 100°F or higher coupled with a rash, earache, sore throat, lethargy, or nausea. Fever may signal a highly contagious infection.
3. a persistent, productive cough and wheezing coupled with a thick or constant nasal discharge.
4. persistent vomiting or diarrhea during the previous night.
5. an undiagnosed rash, especially when there's a fever and behavioral change.
6. pinkeye in which there's a white or yellow discharge, often with matted eyelids after sleep, eye pain, and redness.
7. strep throat/scarlet fever.
8. head lice. Stay home until treated and all nits are removed.
9. chicken pox. Stay home five days after the onset of blisters, or until all pox is scabbed over and dry.[2]

When My Pet Dies

GROWING

Day 1—Matthew had a dog whose name was Timber. Timber was a beautiful Shetland sheepdog who loved Matthew and his family. Matthew and his family loved Timber too. Timber made everyone happy. He could grin and show his teeth when Matthew's mom asked Timber to give them a smile. Timber could sing, and he loved to run through the tall blades of green grass in the fields near Matthew's house in the country. He liked to chase Matthew, and together Timber and Matthew would play for hours.

Timber lived with Matthew and his family for a very long time. Matthew grew up, and Timber grew old. One day Timber woke up and he no longer felt like smiling, singing, or running and playing in the fields. Matthew's family took Timber to the animal doctor. The doctor told Matthew's family that Timber was very sick. He also said Timber would die. That made Matthew and his mom and dad very, very sad. Soon after that, Matthew's family woke up early one morning, and Timber had died. That meant that Timber's body had quit working. Matthew's family cried. They wrapped Timber in his favorite blanket and took him back to the doctor. The doctor said he would take care of Timber's body.

Day 2—Matthew and his family talked about what a good dog Timber had been. They remembered all the fun things they had done with Timber. They framed pictures of Timber and put them around their house. The next day they planted some flowers in their yard to help them remember Timber. Now every day when Matthew's mom waters the flowers, she thanks God for the time her family had with Timber. And she thanks God for making animals for everyone to enjoy.

When a pet dies, God knows you can be very sad, like Matthew's family was. God cares about you, and when you are sad, He wants to help you feel better. You can tell God how you feel, and He will always hear you. Your pet that dies can never come back to live with you again, but God gives us other animals to enjoy. When you and your family are ready to get another pet, you can have fun finding just the right pet for your family. And you know what? You'll love that pet too, and he'll love you right back.

Open the Bible, and read: God made the animals (see Genesis 1:25); God cares for you (see 1 Peter 5:7); and God loves you (see Psalm 107:1).

Say a prayer: Dear God, thank You for making animals and giving us animals to enjoy. Thank You, God, for taking care of my pet when he dies. Amen.

On the Go
- Make a photo collage capturing special times with your pet. Glue photos of your beloved pet onto an 11-by-14-inch piece of poster board. Take your child to help you pick out a frame, and then frame the collage. Put it in a prominent place; and as your child reminisces about his pet, point to the collage and remind him about the fun times he had with the pet.
- Encourage your child to paint a picture of his pet.
- Have a burial service for your child's pet using rocks, wood, flowers, and craft sticks to make a memorial.
- Read *The Dead Bird* by Margaret Wise Brown.

Parent Pointers
Help your child understand that God made the animals and gives us animals to enjoy. Also help him understand that when a pet dies, his body no longer works. Explain that God will take care of the pet when it dies. Provide comforting

163

words and help your child understand that God knows he is sad about his pet dying. Pray with your child, asking God to comfort your family during this time. Reassure your child that the pet's death is not his fault. Let your child tell the pet good-bye if at all possible. Remember the fun times you've had with the pet. Expect regression from your child as this type of trauma can easily disrupt routine and behavior. Be patient. Consider buying another pet.

When Someone Dies

GROWING

Day 1—When someone dies, that means his body no longer works. Have you ever known anyone who died? How did it make you feel? What did you do?

When someone you know dies, it can make you very sad. You may cry. You may see your parents crying too and become afraid or worried. And you may have lots of questions about why a person had to die. You may wonder since that person died if your mother or father will die. You might even worry that you will die.

God made us to live, but our bodies do not keep working forever. So it's part of God's plan that people one day will die. Most people live for a very long time. Your mom and dad want to be there while you grow up, so they want to live for a very long time. You are very young and have a long life to live too.

Day 2—Jesus, God's Son, died on the Cross. But after Jesus died, God raised Him from the dead. Only God's Son could be raised from the dead. Jesus later went to heaven to be with God.

Jesus tells you in the Bible that if you love Him and trust Him and do what He has told you to do, you will go to heaven when you die. That is a promise that Jesus gives to everyone. Isn't that good to know? You do not have to fear dying because when you die, you can go to live with Jesus in heaven.

For now, though, God wants you to live your life like Jesus did. You do that by helping others, being kind to others, showing love, sharing, giving, and praying. Today, how will you show others you are living like Jesus?

Open the Bible, and read: Jesus said, "If you believe in me, when you die, you will come to live with me in heaven" (see John 11:25–26).

Say a prayer: Dear God, thank You for sending Jesus to show us how to live our lives each day. Thank You that we can know that when we die, we can go to live with Jesus in heaven. Amen.

ON THE GO

- Expect young children to have questions about death. Be as honest as possible when answering their questions. In response to questions such as the following, read the suggested Scripture passages and discuss them with your family:

    Does God still love me even though He took my grandfather to live with Him? (Read Romans 8:38–39.)

    Will I ever feel happy again? (Read Romans 8:28.)

    Does God care about how we feel? (Read 1 Corinthians 10:13 and 1 Peter 5:7.)

- Encourage dramatic play with puppets.
- Help your child build with his blocks.
- Let your child act out his feelings. If your child wants to act out "death play," allow him to do so as this helps reduce anxieties.
- Read books such as *Everett Anderson's Goodbye* by Lucille Clifton; *Nana Upstairs and Nana Downstairs* by Tomie dePaola; or *What's Heaven?* by Maria Shriver.
- Make a memory book about the person who died. Include his favorite games, colors, and foods.
- Make a timeline to help your child learn the concept of "a very long time." On the timeline include special events in your child's life, your life, and the lives of your child's grandparents. Help your child to see what things people can do in a lifetime.
- Observe the life cycle of plants with your child.

Moving On

GROWING

Day 1—One day God told Abraham that he had to move. God told him to just go. Abraham had to leave most of his belongings and family behind. He had no time to plan the move. He came home and told his wife, Sarah, what God had told him. It was very hard to do; but because Abraham and Sarah loved God, they did as He told them. They took their sheep and cattle and tents, and many people went with them to help. They traveled for many days and nights and waited for God to let them know just the right place where they were to go. But until they heard from God, they kept moving on.

God promised Abraham and Sarah that if they did what He told them, they would one day have a baby. Abraham and Sarah didn't have any children, but they wanted a baby more than anything. So they trusted God. Soon God led them to the place where they were to stay. The land there was hilly with lots of rock and sand, but they unpacked their belongings and called it home. After they got settled in to their new home, Abraham and Sarah had a baby. God kept His promise to them.

Have you ever had to move? Maybe you moved to another house in the same town; or maybe you even had to move far away to another city, state, or country. Wow! That's a big deal when you are so young. Moving can be very hard for everyone in the family, but it can also be a lot of fun.

Day 2—When you move, you might not like having to pack up your toys, books, games, and clothes. You may worry about what will happen to your things or if you will ever see them again. You may not want to leave your house and especially your room. After all, you had your secret places there where you and your friends played. You had all your favorite colors in that room too.

Moving also means having to leave your friends. You might worry about making new friends. But you can trust God like Abraham and Sarah did. God will be there for you even when you must pack up all your things and make a move. God will help you make new friends when you move. He'll help you find the right house to live in, and even the right room where you and your new friends can play and have fun. God will take care of you, and He promises to give you everything you need. Just like He kept His promise to Abraham and Sarah, He'll keep His promise to you! Nothing is too hard for God, not even when you must move.

Open the Bible, and read: God cares about you (see 1 Peter 5:7); look what God can do (see Luke 1:37); don't worry about things because God will take care of you (see Matthew 6:25); when I am afraid, I will trust in God (see Psalm 56:3).

Say a prayer: Dear God, thank You for taking care of me. I know that You can help me when I must make a move. When I am afraid, I will trust in You, God. Amen.

On the Go
- Prepare your child when you must move. Explain your plans as soon as you know them. The more you prepare, the better.
- Visit the new place where you will be moving. Include the entire family in house hunting when appropriate.
- Take your child to visit his new school prior to his first day.
- Collect brochures or posters about your new town. Find out what's available to explore. Discover new sights there.
- Say good-bye to old friends. Take photos of your child and his friends; put them in a booklet or scrapbook. Take photos of your old house. Look through the booklet as often as your child likes. Talk about old friends and making new friends.

- Help your child make new friends. Register your child in a playgroup, day care, mother's day out, or community program so he can meet other children.
- Prior to moving day, explain how the moving van will come and how things will be packed up in boxes. Help your child role-play loading the van. Work together using blocks to build the new house.
- As you pack for your move, suggest that your child keep several of his favorite toys and not pack those. Allow him to take these toys with him on the way to the new house.
- Encourage your child to help decorate his new room. Let him pick out a new comforter for his bed, paint for his walls, or pictures to display. Show enthusiasm as you unpack his things together. Say: Look what I found. It's your favorite toy car. Where shall we put it?
- Meet the parents of your child's new friends. Invite your child's teacher for dinner. Take time to develop your own new relationships with other parents.
- Draw close as a family, and share your feelings. Read books such as *My Best Friend Moved Away* by Nancy Carlson. Keep your family rituals. Write cards, letters, and emails to send to old friends. Hug and rock a lot.

Manners Matter, Yes They Do!

GROWING

Manners matter. Can you say those words really fast over and over again? "Manners matter, manners matter, manners matter"—yes they do! It's fun to run those words together really fast, isn't it? But manners really do matter. It's important to have good manners, and having good manners is serious business.

Have your parents ever told you to "be polite, and mind your manners"? That can mean they want you to say please and thank you. When you say please and thank you, you are minding your manners. Minding your manners can also mean that you take turns when playing a game with your friend. It might mean that you listen and not talk when someone else is speaking. Or it might mean you say hello to a visitor or someone with whom your parent works. Minding your manners can mean that you hold the door for your grandmother or help your teacher serve the juice during snack time. Saying kind words when talking with your parents, friends, and teachers is also a way to mind your manners. Chewing your food with your mouth closed is another way to mind your manners. So see? There are a lot of different ways to show you have good manners.

When you show that you have good manners, you are being kind, helpful, and caring toward other people. Good manners are also a way of showing your love to others. In the Bible you can read that you are to be kind to others, help others, and love others. When you do these things, you are showing good manners and doing what the Bible says to do.

Now think about it. What will you do to show others that

you have good manners? Now say it again really fast, "Manners matter, manners matter, manners matter"—yes they do!

Open the Bible, and read: Be kind to one another (see Ephesians 4:32); help one another (see Galatians 5:13); and love one another (see 1 John 4:7).

Say a prayer: Dear God, help me to remember that manners matter. Show me how I can be a helper. Teach me to be kind and loving at all times. Amen.

ON THE GO

- Model good manners for your child. When you and your family encounter situations where good manners are not evident, talk about how you could be more courteous, help-ful, loving, and kind in that situation. Talk about using a napkin; chewing food with your mouth closed; and saying please, thank you, and excuse me.
- Sing this song to the tune of "If You're Happy and You Know It" when your child shows good manners.

> *If you want to have good manners, say thank you. (Thank you!)*
>
> *If you want to have good manners, say thank you. (Thank you!)*
>
> *If you want to have good manners, saying please and thank you matters.*
>
> *If you want to have good manners, say thank you. (Thank you!)*

We Are All Different!

GROWING

Day 1—Look in the mirror. Did you know you are one of kind? There is no one exactly like you. God made all kinds of people. In some ways people are alike but in other ways people are different.

You are like others because you have eyes, hair, and skin. But look again. People have different kinds of hair and different colors too. Some of your friends may have curly hair or straight hair, short hair or long hair, blonde hair or brown hair. You and your friends may have different colors of eyes. Some friends may have blue eyes or green eyes or brown eyes. Some of your friends may have dark skin or light skin.

You are like others because you live in God's beautiful world. But look again. People live in many different places around the world. Some friends may live in America, and some may live in Australia, Germany, England, Brazil, Mexico, China, or Kenya.

You are like others because you have to have food and water to live. But look again. Some of your friends eat lots of vegetables, rice, or maybe bananas. Some may eat sushi, while others eat sauerkraut. Some may eat tortillas and others may eat lots of pizza.

You are like others because you wear clothes. But look again. You might wear clothes that are different from some children. Some friends may like to wear hats, caps, or scarves. Others might like to wear pants and a shirt, or some friends may wear long dresses. Some friends may wear tennis shoes and socks, and others might like to wear sandals or flip-flops.

You are like others because you can talk. But listen closely. You speak a different language from some people. Some friends might speak Spanish, German, French, Swahili, or Japanese. Others might speak English, Italian, or Russian.

Day 2—Although each person is different, God loves everyone just the same. God made people to be different. Each person God made is special and unique. That means there is no one exactly like him.

You can learn from others who are different from you. You can learn to say some words in the language they speak, what kind of food they like to eat, what their homeland is like, and what they like to do. You can be friends with people who are different from you.

When you learn to accept other people's differences, you show them respect and love. You are also doing what God says. Do you know what that is? God tells us to love one another.

Open the Bible, and read: Love one another (see 1 John 4:7); God made people (see Genesis 1:27); and God loves us always (see 1 John 4:10).

Say a prayer: Dear God, thank You for making all kinds of people. Thank You for making us different. Help me to learn from other people who are different from me. Help me to be kind and loving towards them. Amen.

On the Go
- Find out more about your family's heritage. Keep a scrapbook with your findings.
- Invite families of other cultures and ethnic groups to your home for dinner or perhaps for a dessert party. Ask each family to bring a dish representative of his culture.
- Avoid using derogatory statements about other ethnic, cultural, or socioeconomic groups.
- Play music from other cultures, nationalities, and races.
- Model tolerance and respect.
- Teach your child to accept himself. Point out what makes him special.
- Help your child cut out paper dolls. Provide markers and

suggest your child color each one and add facial features. Talk about how they are alike and how they are different. Say: God loves everyone.

•Use an inkpad and paper to fingerprint everyone in the family. Point out that no two sets of fingerprints are the exactly the same.

•Intervene when you hear intolerant behavior. Take a stand and let your child know this type of behavior is not appropriate.

•Look in the mirror. Talk about family resemblances. Point out how you are alike and how you are different.

Parent Pointer

Remember to encourage your child to love all people. If a person is doing something you do not approve of, explain to your child that the person's behavior is not acceptable, but that God still loves him and wants us to love him too. Together as a family, pray for that person.

What's Wrong with Cliff?

GROWING

Day 1—Once there was a little boy named Cliff. He came to school like the other children, but he was very different from all the other boys and girls. Cliff had to be in a wheelchair all the time. His legs did not work so he could not walk. Cliff also had trouble talking. His words didn't come out of his mouth clearly like the other boys' and girls' words did. It was hard to know what Cliff was saying.

Sometimes Cliff's body would jerk in all directions, and he wasn't able to sit up in his wheelchair. Sometimes Cliff would slump over in his chair and fall asleep. Cliff was a very nice little boy. But some of the boys and girls in his classroom were afraid of him. They worried that if they played with Cliff they might become like him and have to be in a wheelchair too. One day, Cliff's teacher and he decided to help the class learn more about why Cliff was like he was.

Cliff thought that if he wrote a story about himself and drew pictures to share with the boys and girls, they might better understand. The teacher helped Cliff read the story and show the pictures. The boys and girls learned so much about what Cliff could do. They were glad to learn that although Cliff was in a wheelchair and could not do some things, he could do many things that they couldn't do. That day, Cliff made lots of new friends because the boys and girls were no longer afraid. Now they understood more about Cliff. Each day one of the boys and girls was Cliff's extra-special helper. Everyone liked helping Cliff, and Cliff liked helping the boys and girls too!

Day 2—Have you ever seen someone who was in a wheel-chair? Or have you seen someone who wears glasses or perhaps a hearing aid in his ear? Maybe you've seen some-one who uses crutches to help him walk. Or maybe you've

seen someone wear a brace on his leg. How did it make you feel? Were you afraid of that person? Were you scared that you might become like that person if you played with him?

You have many parts to your body. God made them all. But some people have parts of their bodies that do not work. Do you know how good it makes you feel when you can do something all by yourself? Cliff likes doing things all by himself too, but sometimes he has to have help. Cliff's wheelchair helps him move from place to place. Glasses help people to see better, and hearing aids help them to hear.

God made us all, and He loves us all the same. He wants you to love everyone too. He also wants you to help others. Do you know someone who is in a wheelchair? How can you help that person?

Open the Bible, and read: Love one another (see 1 John 4:7); help one another (see Galatians 5:13); be kind to one another (see Ephesians 4:32); and we are helpers (see 2 Corinthians 1:24).

Say a prayer: God, thank You for making me just like I am. Help me to know how I can be a helper when I see someone who is in a wheelchair. I want to love everyone and not be afraid of others who are different. Help me to show love and kindness to people who cannot see, hear, or walk, and help them to trust in You. Amen.

ON THE GO
- Take your child to a nursing home, perhaps with his friends from church or school. Encourage him to make cards for the friends he meets there.
- When you see someone who is disabled, encourage your child to talk to that person. Answer his questions honestly and reassure your child that he is not responsible for the handicap.
- Work with your church to help meet the special needs of disabled persons.

- Read *What's Wrong with Timmy?* by Maria Shriver. *Heartsongs* and *Journey Through Heartsongs* by Mattie J. T. Stepanek are two other books for older preschoolers and younger children that can help them understand about challenges and feelings a handicapped child must face.
- In restaurants, hotels, schools, and other buildings where you shop or visit, point out design features that help meet the needs of disabled people.
- Talk with your child about the use of closed captioning on television.
- Talk about the Deaf ministry, if your church has one.
- Teach your child some simple sign language phrases such as *I love you.*
- Talk about how blind people read using Braille.
- Focus on what disabled people are able to do.

PARENT POINTER

Disabled and nondisabled children learn and benefit from being around others to see their strengths, courage, and wisdom. Avoid keeping your child from those who are different. Instead encourage him to learn from others' differences.

Computers, TV, and Videos— Oh My!

GROWING

Do you like to watch television? What are your favorite programs? How do you feel after you've watched your favorite program? What TV programs do you not like to watch? How do you decide what to watch? When do you watch TV? Who watches TV with you? Do you like playing video games? Do you use the computer?

The TV, computer, and videos all have some very good programs for a young child like you to watch or play, but they also have some programs that are not very good for young children. Some things that you see on TV or video games can affect how you feel. You might feel happy or sad. You might feel scared or angry after watching a show or playing a video game. Or you might feel all silly and giggly.

Did you know that some things on TV and videos are real, and some things are made up? They are pretend. Do you like to pretend? Well, that's what some people do who are on TV. They pretend to be someone else who does all kinds of things. They are not real things that could really happen. They are just pretending. But it might be kind of hard for you to know what is real on TV and what is not. Has that ever happened to you before?

You can talk to your parents about what kinds of programs you should watch or video games you can play. As a family, watch programs that you all like; and after the program, talk about how it made you feel. Talk about the people in the program, and if what they did in the program was real or not. Your parents will know, and they can help you to learn.

It's always good to have other things to do besides watching TV or playing video and computer games. God made you able to do many different kinds of things. If you are

always watching TV or playing video games, you might not have enough time to do other important things. Have a certain TV and computer time with your family, but be sure to make time for other fun things too. Use your time in ways that please God.

Open the Bible, and read: Obey your parents (see Colossians 3:20).

Say a prayer: Dear God, help me to use my time in ways that make You happy. I want to please You in all that I do and say. Help me to keep learning the difference between real and pretend as I grow. Amen.

On the Go
•Fill a box or a drawer with a variety of special activities for your child. Encourage him to choose an activity from the box and to do it. Keep a list of all the things your child can do, and be enthusiastic as you lead him to try new things. Each day remind your child that God made him to do many things.
•Make up your own family TV programs. Cut a large box to make a puppet stage and use hand puppets to present your own special TV show. Or, get an even larger box to use in creating your own TV shows, with family members as actors inside the box. Use music and dance, poems, stories, or songs. Have a TV cook show and make your favorite dish on TV.

R-E-S-P-O-N-S-I-B-I-L-I-T-Y

GROWING

Day 1 —Can you say the word *responsibility? Responsibility.* As you grow, you are learning many new words. Some of them are quite big words too, aren't they? Responsibility means that you are learning to do things all by yourself. You might even do them without anyone telling you to do them. That is really being responsible.

When you brush your teeth, you are being responsible. When you help your teacher at cleanup time, you are being responsible. When you put away your toys at home, you are being responsible too. Do you know that the things you do affect other people around you? Have you ever hurt someone's feelings? Did you tell them you were sorry? When you hurt someone and you say you are sorry for what you did, you are being responsible. When you tell the truth, you are being responsible.

Day 2—Everyone has a job that he must do. Moms and dads may go to work to earn money for the family. You and your brothers and sisters may go to school to learn many new things. When you do the best you can at whatever your job is, you are being responsible.

Jesus was a responsible person too. He always told the truth. He showed love and kindness to others. He told people that God loved them. Jesus did good things. He was a helper, kind and good. As you keep growing and learning, you can become more and more like Jesus. You can become more responsible as you grow too. Isn't that a good feeling to know you can be like Jesus and be responsible? You can be responsible for yourself. And one day you will become responsible for others too.

Open the Bible, and read: Jesus went about doing good things (Acts 10:38); we are helpers (see 2 Corinthians 1:24); and help one another (see Galatians 5:13)

Say a prayer: Dear God, thank You that every day I am growing and learning to be more responsible. Help me to do good things and make good choices. Help me to do my best and trust You even when I do things wrong or I forget to do things. Thank You for loving me all the time. Amen.

ON THE GO
•Make a Job Chart. List names and responsibilities for each family member on the chart. Put a check mark beside each job when the person responsible has completed it. Take photos of your child helping, tending to his needs, or doing chores. Place these on the chart. At the end of the week, take your child to his favorite restaurant to celebrate his taking responsibility.

PARENT POINTER
Be clear about roles and allow preschoolers to learn from their mistakes. Use open-ended questions such as What happens if you do not do your job? or Why is it important for each person to do his part? Use positive words when encouraging your child to behave responsibly.[3]

When People Do Bad Things

GROWING

Day 1—Do you ever wonder why people do bad things? Does it scare you? Do you feel unsafe when you see things or hear about things that are bad? Maybe you know someone who has done bad things. You might be afraid of that person. You might worry and feel very sad or angry. You might have headaches or stomachaches. Someone may have even hurt you. If that has happened to you and you have not told anyone, you need to tell your mom or dad or another adult. This person will help you because she cares for you and loves you. She will be able to help you feel better.

You may have noticed that your parents also get sad and upset when they see people doing bad things. Did you know that even grown-ups do not know exactly why people do bad things or why some bad things have to happen? You and your parents can talk with each other about how you feel when you see or hear about people who do bad things. You may want your mom and dad to hold you and hug you when you feel scared. And guess what? They may need for you to hold them too! When bad things happen, it's OK to feel sad or scared. God will help you and your mom and dad to feel better. Your mom and dad will do everything they can to help keep you safe.

Day 2—You might wonder how you can love someone who does bad things. God wants you to love people no matter what they do. Did you know you can still love people who do bad things? You don't love the bad things the people do. Of course not! God doesn't either, but He still loves the people. God is love, and He says in the Bible that He will love us always no matter what. God will love you always too.

Open the Bible, and read: God loves us always (see Psalm 107:1) and I will not be afraid because God is with me (see Psalm 23:4).

Say a prayer: Dear God, thank You for loving everyone always. When I am scared and sad, help me to remember that You are always with me. Thank You for my family. They always make me feel safe. Amen.

On the Go

- Play relaxing music as you ride in the car or at home while holding your child. Read comforting books such as *The Rainbow Fish* by Marcus Pfister, *The Owl Who Was Afraid of the Dark* by Jill Tomlinson, or *Goodnight Moon* by Margaret Wise Brown. Rub your child's neck and back at naptime or bedtime to help soothe his tensions.
- Work together as a family on projects to help people who are victimized by bad things. Draw a picture, make a card, or save money to give to these people. Lead your child to pray daily for these people and their families.
- Tell your child every day, "I love you!" Say it often!

Parent Pointers

Remind your child that the bad actions of a few people should never make them afraid of all people or whole groups of people. Help your child learn that bad actions taken by a few people cannot begin to match the great things that good people can do.

When your child sees someone doing bad things, talk to him about what has happened. Also talk about TV programs, videos, movies, or computer games when your child sees someone doing bad things. Avoid letting your child play violent games and watching violence on TV.

Taking Care of the Earth

GROWING

Day 1—God gives you good things to enjoy. The earth and all that is in it are yours to enjoy. These things are gifts from God. Taking care of the earth is very important. God wants you to do your part to help keep the earth clean, safe, and a happy place to live.

One way to help take care of the earth is to recycle. Recycle means you can use something again and again. You can help recycle papers, plastic cartons and containers, glass, boxes, and aluminum cans. You can collect some of these at your house and then take them to a recycling center. Your city might have someone who comes to your house to collect recyclable items. When these items get picked up, they are taken to a recycling plant. There the materials are broken down and then remade so they can be used again. When you use something again and again, you help take care of the earth.

Day 2—Another way to take care of the earth is to put trash in its proper place. Throwing trash on the ground makes the earth look dirty and takes away from all its beauty. You can put trash in a container. If you are riding in your car, you can put trash in a litterbag. When the car stops, you can empty the litterbag into a bigger trashcan. If you are playing on the playground, you can put any trash you have or find in a trashcan. You can help pick up trash around your house, neighborhood, or church.

Helping to keep the air clean is another way to take care of the earth. Sometimes the air you breathe gets very dirty. When the air is dirty, people have trouble breathing, and sometimes they get very sick from dirty air. Cars and factories can cause the air to get dirty. Do you know how?

Sometimes they make fumes and smoke that go into the air. Sometimes these are harmful if people breathe them.

Thank God for everything He has given you to enjoy on the earth. Ask Him to show you ways to take care of the earth so you can enjoy it even more.

Open the Bible, and read: Everything God made was very good (see Genesis 1:31).

Say a prayer: God, thank You for the earth. Show me ways that I can take care of the earth and enjoy all the wonderful things You give me to enjoy. Amen.

On the Go

- Become a family that recycles. Place several large plastic tubs in a convenient place in your house. Label each tub with one of the following: *Paper, Glass, Plastic, Aluminum.* Ask your child to help you place recyclable items into each tub. Talk to your child about the items and how they can be used again. Take your child to a recycling center to help him learn more about how these items are reused.
- Teach your child to help take care of the grounds in your neighborhood, church, or community. Encourage him to pick up trash and to place his trash in the proper place.
- As you are on the go, talk about fresh air and how healthy it is to get fresh air. Feel the wind as you walk together. Learn the names of trees, flowers, and wildflowers. As you drive through state parks or in the countryside, take photos of God's beautiful world. Talk about endangered species. Praise God for His creation.
- Feed the animals in your backyard. Help your child make a bird feeder. Take a medium-sized pinecone and cover it with either peanut butter or shortening. (Lard works even better.) Roll in birdseed until the pinecone is covered. Tie the bird feeder to a tree branch. Enjoy watching the birds in your backyard.[4]

Mom and Dad Go to Work

GROWING

Day 1—Many boys and girls just like you have moms and dads who work outside of the home. Does your mom have a job where she must go work? Does your dad? What do they do? Have you seen where they work? Why do you think your mom and dad must work? Did you know that working is one of the ways that your mom and dad show you that they care?

You see, your parents must work so they can have enough money for your family. Many times both a mom and a dad must work so the family will have enough money. Moms and dads earn money so families can buy food and clothes and have a place to live. Moms and dads may also work because it makes them happy to use the skills God gives them to help others.

Day 2—Sometimes your mom or dad may travel in their work. This means they might have to be gone for a few days or weeks. If your mom or dad travels, you may worry that they won't come back or you may miss them very much. Did you know they miss you too when they travel? They can't wait to get back home to see you.

Work is a part of God's plan. When moms and dads have jobs outside of the home, it is important for everyone in the family to help each other. Each person can do his part around the house to help with chores. As you grow, you are able to do many things that help at home. The Bible tells you to work together and to help each other. Helping each other and working together is what God wants you to do.

One day when you are older, you will probably have a job too. What would you like your job to be when you grow up?

Open the Bible, and read: We work together (see 1 Corinthians 3:9); we are helpers (see 2 Corinthians 1:24); and help one another (see Galatians 5:13).

Say a prayer: Dear God, thank You for my parents' jobs. Please help them in their work to do a good job. Thank You for police officers, firefighters, doctors, nurses, taxi drivers, teachers, and pastors. Thank You that people have jobs to make our lives better. Amen.

On the Go

• Help your child learn more about your job. Take your child to work and let him see where you are during the day. Help him to understand about the kind of work you do. Lead him to role-play you going to work and doing your job.
• When you return from work each day, hug, hold, or rock your child. Tell him how much you missed him. Let your child help with dinner preparations as you talk and spend time catching up.
• If your job requires travel, send cards, letters, or emails to your child. Call your child daily. Prior to leaving, make a cassette recording of you reading your child's favorite book. Leave "love" notes for your child to find while you are away. Arrange for someone to videotape special events or school plays that you miss. When you return, spend time watching these together as a family.
• Spend extra time with your child on your days off and weekends. Give him your undivided attention.[5]

No More Jobs!

GROWING

You have learned that moms and dads sometimes must go to work so they can have enough money for their families. Do you remember how the money your parents earn helps your family? What can your family do with the money?

It's good when moms and dads have jobs to help earn money. But there are some moms and dads who need jobs but don't have them. Sometimes finding a job can be quite hard. Sometimes the place where a mom or dad was working may no longer need them to do the work. Then they must leave where they were working. When a mom or dad does not have a job, their families can be scared and worred. Everyone in the family might worry if they will have money to buy food or clothes. They may worry about how they will pay for other things their family needs.

How would you feel if your mom or dad no longer had a job making money for the family? Would you be scared? Would you be worried? Would you be sad? You may not feel like doing things you used to like doing. You may not want to play with your friends. You may not want to go to your school. You may get angry easily at your friends and even your family. These feelings are OK, and God knows how you feel. You can talk to God and ask God to help you and your family. God cares about you and He wants to help you. God will take care of all your needs.

Open the Bible, and read: God cares for you (see 1 Peter 5:7).

Say a prayer: Dear God, sometimes I worry about my family (or my friend's family) because Dad and Mom do not have a job. Please help them to find a job so we can have enough money to buy food and clothes. Thank You, God, for caring and for helping my family. Amen.

On the Go

- If your family is experiencing job loss, help your child cope with his feelings by praying with him daily.
- Continue to have fun with extended family, grandparents, aunts, uncles, and cousins. Let them keep your child when you job hunt, prepare and send résumés, etc.
- Talk honestly with your child about how he can help when you or someone you know has lost a job. Avoid burdening your child with things he cannot understand.
- Talk to your child's teachers and help them understand his fears.
- Praise your child even more when he helps during an employment loss. Make every effort to show more love and affection for him. Give him lots of hugs and kisses.
- Help other families who are experiencing job loss by inviting them to your home for dinner or taking them dinner one evening each week.
- Label several boxes with the words *Clothes, Food, Toys.* Suggest your child collect items to place in each box. Take filled boxes to homeless shelters, community centers, church, or a needy family.
- Call a homeless shelter. Find out ways your family (including your preschooler) can "adopt" another family to help. Offer to keep their children while they look for jobs. Keep in touch with the family through letters and cards.
- When you see a homeless person on the side of the road, stop and buy him a snack, lunch, or bottled water. Give him a clean blanket.

Uh-oh, I Said a Dirty Word

GROWING

Day 1—Sometimes you might say something or use a word that your parents have told you not to say. They might say that the word you used was a "dirty word," or a "bad word." If you've said a dirty word, you are not alone. Your friends have probably done this too; but that doesn't make it right, does it?

You might have said the word because you heard it on TV or at the movies. Or maybe you heard someone else say the word. You were just copying what someone else said. If your parents or teachers tell you that a word is a dirty word, you must try hard not to say the word again. It could make people around you upset; and you don't want to upset people, do you? No, of course not! You want to treat others with kindness, love, and respect. You want to do that because that is how Jesus said we should treat others. You want to be like Jesus and do the things Jesus tells us to do in the Bible.

Day 2—In the Bible, Jesus tells us to treat others like we want to be treated. The Bible also tells us to be kind to one another and to love others. How do you like to be treated? Do you like to be treated with kindness? Do you like for people to say nice words to you? Did you know everyone likes to be treated with kindness and have nice words said to him?

You have learned that the things you do affect other people around you. The words you say also affect people around you. Be careful about the words you choose to say. If you slip and say a dirty word, remember you can say you are sorry for saying it. You can choose good words to say. Choosing good words to say will make you and others feel happy and good inside. And that's such a good feeling!

Open the Bible, and read: Use good words when you speak (see Proverbs 16:21); and do not say bad things about others, but treat others like you want to be treated (see Matthew 7:1–2).

Say a prayer: Dear God, forgive me when I say unkind things or words that hurt others. Help me to choose good words to say. I want to say good words that show others kindness, love, and respect. Amen.

ON THE GO

•Your child will sometimes hear words that you do not want him to say. Help him to learn that certain words can hurt others or upset other people. Remind him every day to choose his words carefully. As you are on the go, sing the following song to the tune of "(Here We Go 'Round) the Mulberry Bush."

> *Here I go choosing good words to say.*
> *Good words to say.*
> *Good words to say,*
> *Here I go choosing good words to say.*
> *Being kind and loving every day.*
>
> *I will treat others in such a good way.*
> *Such a good way.*
> *Such a good way.*
> *I will treat others in such a good way.*
> *Being like Jesus every day!*

I Like Getting an Allowance

GROWING

Day 1—Do you get an allowance? Getting an allowance might be a way your parents help you learn about money. You might help out around the house by doing certain chores such as setting the table, putting away your toys, dusting, or folding the laundry. When you earn money for doing your chores, you learn that hard work pays off.

What can you do with the money you get? The first thing you should do is to give some of the money you've earned to God. God tells us in the Bible that this is important. You can place money in the offering plate at church or in your bank in your Sunday School or missions room. This money you give to your church helps people in your church, missionaries, and needy people. That is what God means when He tells us to give some of the money to Him. He means that He wants us to give money that will help other people.

Day 2—What else can you do with your money? You can save it and maybe spend it later. You can use some of it to buy presents for your friends or family or even yourself.

Sometimes you might want to buy everything you see. Have you ever been to the toy store and wanted to buy something, but your mom or dad said you could not? Most people cannot buy everything they want. God wants us to spend our money in smart ways. He does not want us to waste it.

Your parents will help you to have everything you need. They can help you learn how to spend your money in ways that please God.

Open the Bible, and read: I will bring an offering to church (see Malachi 3:10).

Say a prayer: Dear God, thank You for the money that I earn. Teach me ways to spend and use my money in ways that will make You happy. Amen.

On the Go

- By the age of three, a child can begin learning about money. Consider giving your child an allowance. Help him to save some of the money and give it to church. Suggest your child make a bank using a clean plastic tub with a lid, such as one that margarine comes in. Cut a slit in the lid of the plastic tub. Lead your child to find pictures from old Sunday School literature or magazines showing people helping others. Help your child cut out the pictures and glue them to the tub. As you work on the bank, talk about the importance of giving money to help others.
- Play store with your child. Use a toy cash register and play money (if you do not want to use real money). Role-play shopping and talk about spending money in smart ways.
- Take your child on a short shopping trip for groceries, toiletries, or his clothing. Show him the prices on each item and compare prices. (Keep in mind a child this age will have a short attention span, so choose one or two items in one shopping trip to compare.)

Teasing and Bullying

GROWING

Have you ever been teased? Or has someone ever pushed you around and made you do things you didn't want to do? You may have done those things because you were scared or maybe afraid of that person.

As you grow, you will sometimes meet people who tease or bully you. Sometimes when people tease you, they may just be trying to have fun and play with you. Other times, though, they may really mean to hurt your feelings. They might call you a name or they might laugh at you and make fun of something you did. They may say they are not going to play with you if you don't do things their way. Sometimes they may hit, kick, or push you. When they do these things, you may feel like being all alone or crying. You may feel very sad and unhappy. Did you know that when a person teases or bullies you, he usually does this because he doesn't understand things; or maybe he even feels scared, alone, or afraid?

When you are teased or bullied, you can tell Jesus all about it. He understands because He was teased and bullied too. A group of people called Pharisees always tried to find something wrong with what Jesus did. They called Him names because they did not like Him. They wanted to discourage Him. But Jesus went right on doing what God wanted Him to do. Do you know what else Jesus did? He prayed for those people who made fun of Him and teased Him. That's what Jesus wants you to do too.

When people tease or bully you, you can pray for them. You can also tell your parents or teachers and they can help you too. When someone teases or bullies you, it is not your fault. God cares for you and He also cares for those who are doing the teasing and bullying. God wants everyone to be kind to each other and not hurt each other.

Open the Bible, and read: Treat others as you want to be treated (Luke 6:31), and be kind to one another (see Ephesians 4:32).

Say a prayer: Dear God, when I'm teased or bullied by someone, help me to be kind. They may be afraid or worried. Show me ways that I can help them. Teach me to love others like You do even when they are people I don't really like. Amen.

ON THE GO
•When your child is teased or bullied, help him draw a song. Provide paper and markers and soothing music as the child draws.
•Suggest that your child paint a picture. Or, give him some clay to pound, and tell him it's OK to pound it hard!
•Let your child help you squeeze lemons and make lemonade.
•Encourage your child to move creatively to music. Help him make up a song about how he is feeling or pound on a drum.
•When your child is bullied or teased, praise him even more than usual for his accomplishments.

PARENT POINTERS
Help your child know that when he is a victim of teasing or bullying, it is not his fault. Talk to your child about the problem, and pray with him about the situation.

Inform your child's teacher about the problem.

Get to know the child who is doing the teasing or bullying. Talk to his parents.

Keep Trying

GROWING

Sometimes you might try to do new things such as playing a game, tying your shoes, writing your name, learning a new song, riding a bicycle, or making up your bed. Trying new things can be fun, but it might be hard too. Have you ever tried doing something and it was just too hard? Did you feel like giving up and not trying again?

In the Bible you can read about a man named Nehemiah. Nehemiah was very smart and he always prayed. He tried to do what God wanted him to do. He knew that God wanted him, with the help of others, to rebuild a wall around the city of Jerusalem. Now Nehemiah had never built a wall before. He and his helpers carefully planned how they would begin their new task. Some people did not want Nehemiah to rebuild the wall, so they did everything they could to discourage Nehemiah. They made fun of Nehemiah and laughed at what he was trying to do. These people became angry and said mean and cruel things to Nehemiah and his helpers. Nehemiah did not give up, though. He prayed and asked God to help him. Nehemiah did everything to please God. It was not easy, but Nehemiah kept on trying. With hard work and doing what God wanted, Nehemiah and the others were able to rebuild the wall around the city.

Every day you are growing and learning to do new things. Learning to do something well takes time and lots of practice, so don't give up. With God's help, you will be able to do many things. Just keep trying!

Open the Bible, and read: Never give up (see Galatians 6:9).

Say a prayer: Dear God, sometimes doing new things can be really hard. I feel like giving up and not trying again. Help me to keep trying no matter what people say or do. Help me to do what You want me to. Amen.

ON THE GO

- Teach your child the words to a new song or a poem. Sing a short part of the song and repeat it often. Help your child to learn one part of the song at a time. Sing as you ride in the car, take walks, wait for the bus or taxi, or do chores around the house. Encourage your child to keep trying to learn the new words to the song.

- Help your child make stilts. Use two coffee cans, long pieces of string, and scissors. Turn the cans upside down. Use the scissors to punch holes in two sides of both cans. Help your child tread a piece of string through the holes. Tie the string together making it about waist high to your child. Encourage your child to walk on the stilts. If he has trouble at first, suggest he keep trying. (Supervise carefully.)[6]

What Is Terrorism?
Why Do We Have War?

GROWING

Day 1—On TV you may have seen planes crashing into buildings and the buildings falling to the ground. You may also have seen people running away from the buildings. They were covered with dust and screaming and crying as they ran. You know some things on TV are not real. Your mother and father may have told you that when these planes hit the buildings and they fell to the ground, this was real. This was a very sad thing to happen and it was also very scary.

You probably asked your mom and dad why someone would do such a terrible thing. Sometimes some people get very angry with other people who do not agree with them or think like they think. These people have not learned how to get along with other people. Sometimes these people do things that hurt other people. The people who hurt others live in different places. They may have white skin, brown skin, or very dark skin. They may have blond hair, brown hair, or red hair. They come in all shapes and sizes. But there is one thing that you must remember. There are more people in this world who do good things than those who do bad things. Terrorists are a few people who do terrible things to hurt others because they want to scare people. They want people to do things their way.

Day 2—Our country, America, is a free country. Living in a free country means you can say what you think, pray and worship God wherever you want to, and feel safe. But when bad things happen, you may not feel safe; and that may make you worry.

Did you know America has men and women who help keep you and your family safe? These men and women work in the military. The military is the marines, army, navy, and air force. These men and women help protect our country from those who want to hurt or scare people. You may know someone in the military. Maybe your mom or dad is in the military.

God wants everyone to live in peace. He wants people everywhere to love each other and help each other. You and your family can pray for people everywhere to learn to love each other. You and your family can also pray for the men and women who are in the military. You can even pray for those people who do bad things. Jesus prayed for people who said and did bad things to Him. Spend time with your family praying for your country and its leaders. Pray for one another.

Open the Bible, and read: Pray for one another (see James 5:16); love each other (see John 15:17); God hears us when we pray (see 1 John 5:14); and Jesus prayed (see Matthew 14:23).

Say a prayer: Dear God, I feel very scared when I hear about terrible things that happen. Help me to trust in You when I am afraid. I know that you made all people. I know that You love all people too. Please help people who do bad things to know about You so that they can learn to love others and not do the bad things anymore. Amen.

ON THE GO

- Offer reassurance in a calm and soothing way to your child when he is frightened. Give lots of hugs and smiles, and hold hands often. Tell your child that you will take care of him every day.
- Avoid overloading your child with too much information. Answer his questions. Be there to listen and take your cues from your child.

- During frightening or upsetting times, make sure that your young child keeps his usual routines. Help him make decisions when he cannot handle choices.
- Make sure your child gets enough exercise, sleep, and nutritious meals and snacks.
- Recognize that a child's emotional responses will be quite different from those of an adult during difficult situations. Accept a child's responses to terrible events, even silliness.
- Avoid pressuring a child to talk about the event if he is not ready. When he is ready, help him to know that God and you will help keep him safe.
- Avoid watching repeated TV broadcasts of horrific events. When young children watch events such as the planes crashing into the buildings over and over again, they think this is actually happening over and over again. They do not know that it is being replayed on TV.
- Read books together such as Nancy Carlson's *How About a Hug?* Encourage pretend play about troubling events; and have time for relaxation as preschoolers play with sand, water, and clay, or draw and paint pictures.
- Help your child respect diversity.
- Watch for any behavior changes such as more clinging, crying, or wanting to be alone; and changes in sleep or eating patterns. Talk to teachers and counselors. Seek professional help if necessary.[7]

BIBLIOGRAPHY

Brazelton, T. Berry, MD, and Joshua D. Sparrow, MD. *Touchpoints Three to Six: Your Child's Emotional and Behavioral Development.* Cambridge, MA: Perseus Books, 2001.

Brazelton, T. Berry, MD, and Stanley I. Greenspan, MD. *The Irreducible Needs of Children: What Every Child Must Have to Grow, Learn, and Flourish.* Cambridge, MA: Perseus Books, 2001.

Burdeshaw, Jane. *Music for Today's Preschoolers.* Birmingham, AL: New Hope Publishers, 1996.

Gaither, Gloria, and Shirley Dobson. *Let's Hide the Word: Joyful Ways to Build Biblical Principles in Your Home.* Dallas: Word Publishing, 1994.

_____. *Let's Make a Memory: Great Ideas for Building Family Traditions and Togetherness.* Dallas: Word Publishing, 1994.

Lewis, Rose A. *I Love You Like Crazy Cakes.* Boston: Little, Brown and Company, 2000.

Miller, Susan A., EdD. "Learning to Cooperate." *Scholastic Early Childhood Today* (November/December 2000).

_____. "Learning to Be Responsible." *Scholastic Early Childhood Today* (January 2001).

_____. "Honesty, What Can You Do?" *Scholastic Early Childhood Today* (February 2001).

Owen, Barbara. *Look, I'm Cooking: Simple Recipes for Preschoolers.* Birmingham, AL: New Hope Publishers, 1993.

Reeves, Rhonda. *200+ Ways to Care for Preschoolers.* Birmingham, AL: New Hope Publishers, 1997.

Reeves, Rhonda, comp. *Tackling Tough Issues.* Birmingham, AL: New Hope Publishers, 1999.

Schomburg, Roberta, and Patricia Honisek. *Mister Rogers' Plan and Play Book.* 4th ed. Pittsburgh: Family Communications, Inc., 1983.

Schwartz, Mike. "School or Sickbed?" *Scottsdale Tribune,* January 22, 2002.

Stonehouse, Catherine. *Joining Children on the Spiritual Journey: Nurturing a Life of Faith.* Grand Rapids, MI: Baker Books, 1998.

RESOURCES

Brown, Margaret Wise. *The Dead Bird.* New York: William Morrow and Company, 2002.

_____. *Goodnight Moon.* Reissue ed. New York: Harpercollins Juvenile Books, 1991.

Carlson, Nancy. *How About a Hug?* New York: Viking Children's Books, 2001.

_____. *My Best Friend Moved Away.* New York: Viking Children's Books, 2001.

Christenson, Evelyn. *What Happens When Children Pray.* Colorado Springs: Chariot Victor Publishing, 1997.

Clifton, Lucille. *Everett Anderson's Goodbye*. 1st ed. New York: Henry Holt and Company, 1983.

Curtis, Jamie Lee. *Today I Feel Silly and Other Moods That Make My Day*. New York: Harpercollins Juvenile Books, 1998.

dePaola, Tomie. *Nana Upstairs and Nana Downstairs*. New York: Putnam Publishing Group, 1973.

Hackerott, Michelle Dawn. *Who Am I?* Birmingham, AL: New Hope Publishers, 2000.

Langley, Judy. *God's World and Me from A–Z*. Birmingham, AL: New Hope Publishers, 2000.

Law, Jennifer. *I Like to Go to Church*. Birmingham, AL: Woman's Missionary Union, 2000.

_____. *Around the World*. Birmingham, AL: Woman's Missionary Union, 2002.

_____. *In My Community*. Birmingham, AL: Woman's Missionary Union, 2002.

Quantrell, Angie. *I Can Pray*. Birmingham, AL: Woman's Missionary Union, 2000.

Reeves, Rhonda. *Good Things Jesus Did*. Birmingham, AL: Woman's Missionary Union, 1999.

_____. *Families Are Special*. Birmingham, AL: Woman's Missionary Union, 2000.

_____. *God's Beautiful World*. Birmingham, AL: Woman's Missionary Union, 2001.

_____. *MYSELF*. Birmingham, AL: Woman's Missionary Union, 2001.

Reeves, Rhonda, and Jennifer Law. *I Can Help Others*; Birmingham, Alabama; Woman's Missionary Union, 1998.

_____. *Tell Me About God*. Birmingham, AL: Woman's Missionary Union, 1998.

_____. *Thank You, God, for My Bible*. Birmingham, AL: Woman's Missionary Union, 1999.

Rock, Lois. *The Ten Commandments for Children*. Colorado Springs: Chariot Victor Publishing, 1995.

Shriver, Maria. *What's Heaven?* New York: Golden Books Publishing Company, 1999.

_____. *What's Wrong with Timmy?* Boston: Little Brown Children's Books, 2001.

Silverstein, Shel. *The Giving Tree*. New York: Harpercollins Juvenile Books, 1986.

Stepanek, Mattie J. T. *Heartsongs*. New York: Hyperion, 2002.

_____. *Journey Through Heartsongs*. Alexandria, VA: Vacation Spot Publishing, 2001.

Tomlin, Carolyn. *More Alike than Different*. Birmingham, AL: Woman's Missionary Union, 2000.

Tomlinson, Jill. *The Owl Who Was Afraid of the Dark*. Cambridge, MA: Candlewick Press, 2001.

Notes

INTRODUCTION

[1]Catherine Stonehouse, *Joining Children on the Spiritual Journey: Nurturing a Life of Faith* (Grand Rapids, MI: Baker Books 1998), 133.

[2]Ibid., 139.

PART I

[1]The special hug idea was adapted from *The Mailbox, Preschool, 2000–2001 Yearbook* (Greensboro, NC: The Education Center, Inc., 2001), 40.

[2]The bug catcher idea was adapted from "Discoveries," *Everyday TLC*, July 30, 2001.

[3]The woodworking idea is from *Mr. Rogers' Plan and Play Book*, 4th ed. (Pittsburgh: Family Communications, Inc., 1983), 323.

PART II

[1]The Bible drainer display idea was adapted from *The Mailbox, Preschool*, December/January 2001–2002, 45.

[2]The name crackers idea was adapted from "Getting Ready for Fall," *Everyday TLC*, August 27, 2001.

[3]The potato chip can idea was adapted from *The Mailbox, Preschool*, February/March 2001, 23.

[4]The pretend wedding idea was adapted from *Mister Rogers' Plan and Play Book*, 4th ed. (Pittsburgh: Family Communications, Inc., 1983), 315.

[5]The good deeds chart idea was adapted from "Honesty, What Can You Do?" *Scholastic Early Childhood Today*, February 2001, 29.

Part III

[1]The salad idea is from "Host a Fall Foods Family Activity," in brochure "Sharing Nutrition Messages with Families," Fall 2001, produced by Celebrate Healthy Living, a Scholastic Program Sponsored by Dannon Institute (www.dannon-institute.org).

[2]The dinner party idea is from Gloria Gaither and Shirley Dobson, *Let's Make a Memory* (Dallas: Word Publishing, 1994), 161.

[3]The references for worshiping together as a family are from Gloria Gaither and Shirley Dobson, *Let's Hide the Word* (Dallas: Word Publishing, 1994), 89.

[4]This fingerplay is taken from "Fingerplays for Fun," *Everyday TLC*, October 16, 2000.

[5]The bubble mixture idea is taken from "Blowing Bubbles," *Everyday TLC*, May 1, 2001.

Part IV

[1]The head, shoulders, knees, and toes idea was adapted from Valerie Corbeille, "Head, Shoulders, Knees, and Toes," *The Mailbox*, Preschool, August/September 2001, 25.

[2]The I Am Special book idea was adapted from "Self Esteem," *Everyday TLC*, January 21, 2002.

[3]The snack pack server idea was adapted from "Summer Reading," *Everyday TLC*, June 25, 2001.

[4]The fabric cards idea is from Roberta Schomburg and Patricia Honisek, *Mister Rogers' Plan and Play Book*, 5th ed. (Pittsburgh: Family Communications, Inc., 1995), 214.

[5]The cookie idea was adapted from Barbara Owen, *Look, I'm Cooking* (Birmingham, AL: New Hope Publishers, 1993), 42.

[6]The ideas in "When I Get Mad" are from Rhonda Reeves, comp., *Tackling Tough Issues* (Birmingham: AL: New Hope Publishers, 1999), 65–76.

[7]The picture circle idea is from "When's Mommy Coming?" *The Mailbox*, Preschool, August/September 2001, 16.

[8]The Newcomb idea was adapted from *Scholastic Early Childhood Today*, April 1999, 55.

[9]Parent Pointer on cooperation was adapted from Susan A. Miller, EdD, "Learning to Cooperate," *Scholastic Early Childhood Today*, November/December 2000, 41.

[10]Ellen Booth Church, "How Children Solve Problems," *Scholastic Early Childhood Today*, April 1999, 36–37.

Part V
[1]The parent and child cookbook idea is from "Feelings," *Everyday TLC*, May 28, 2001.

[2]The health information is from Mike Schwartz, "School or Sickbed?" *Scottsdale Tribune*, January 22, 2002.

[3]Susan A. Miller, EdD, and Ellen Booth Church, "Learning to Be Responsible," *Scholastic Early Childhood Today*, January 2001, 32–35.

[4]The bird feeder activity is adapted from "Fall Walks and Activities," *Everyday TLC*, November 6, 2000.

[5]The ideas about spending time with children were adapted from T. Berry Brazelton, MD, and Joshua D. Sparrow, MD, *Touchpoints Three to Six: Your Child's Emotional and Behavioral Development* (Cambridge, MA: Perseus Books, 2001), 466–70.

[6]The stilts idea was adapted from Roberta Schomburg and Patricia Honisek, *Mister Rogers' Plan and Play Book*, 4th ed. (Pittsburgh: Family Communications, Inc., 1983), 285, 280.

[7]The ideas about helping a child cope with frightening times are from Jane M. Farish, "Helping Young Children in Frightening Times," *Young Children*, November 2001, 6–7; adapted from "When Disaster Strikes: Helping Young Children Cope" (National Association for the Education of Young Children brochure).

Also by Rhonda Reeves

Great ideas for caring for your preschooler.

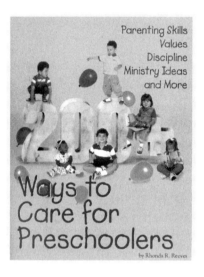

Parenting Skills
Values
Discipline
Ministry Ideas
and More

Ways to
Care for
Preschoolers
by Rhonda R. Reeves

1-56309-208-5

200+ Ways to Care for Preschoolers provides helpful hints for parenting, instilling Christian values, establishing discipline techniques, and introducing the concepts of ministry. Packed with practical advice and fun activities, this book is a great resource for parents, teachers, and caregivers.

Available in Christian bookstores everywhere.

New Hope
Publishers

Equipping You to Share the Hope of Christ